Date Due

APR 04 1984			

© THE BAKER & TAYLOR CO.

More For Your Money

More For
Your Money

How to Increase Your Spending Power
Up to 20% Without Increasing Your Income

Mary Bowen Hall

1981 Houghton Mifflin Company Boston

Library of Congress Cataloging in Publication Data

Hall, Mary Bowen.
  More for your money.

  1. Home economics — Accounting. 2. Budgets, Personal.
I. Title.
TX326.H24   640'.42   81-2923
ISBN 0-395-31293-0   AACR2

Printed in the United States of America

V 10 9 8 7 6 5 4 3 2 1

Contents

List of Worksheets

Acknowledgments

I've had lots of help.

I've been helped all along by a number of people who've greeted my ideas with enthusiasm and told me the specific ways in which these ideas have helped them. I've consulted experts, too. You will see many of their names in the pages of this book.

Three experts have played particularly important roles. Dr. William Buckner of Long Beach State University gave a talk several years ago that set me to thinking and was a major influence in the chain of ideas that led to the development of this book. He also worked very closely with me as I wrote Chapter Five. Dr. Henry Lindgren, professor of psychology at San Francisco State University, provided thoughtful help and insights. Dr. Herbert Harris, counselor in marriage and family relations, validated for me from his extensive experience my ideas about how people behave in relation to money.

Friends of mine who are writers and editors have been able to offer help on two levels — professional and personal. And those people you will come to know in the last section of the book as Debra L. and Homer and Maureen P. not only shared the details of their dreams and finances but also gave freely of their time.

Perhaps the most extensive help has come from my husband. During the past year he's lived with both me and my book. He's held my hand when that was important but been an outspoken critic, too, when that was needed.

PART I

Understand

Your Spending Style

1.

Spending Power Basics

THE UNITED STATES is a nation of consumers. You and I — all of us — misuse our spending power and waste a great deal of money because we don't spend it for what we really want. We often do as we are sold. Most of us are ignorant of the money traps that can ensnare our income.

Here are some of our typical mistakes:

* We don't take the time to figure out why we are buying what we buy. In fact, we may not have decided what we really want to have and do.
* We don't consider alternatives to buying "things," such as spending for services or for leisure-enhancing skills.
* We don't understand money traps — neither the ones laid by others nor the ones that we set for ourselves.
* We don't know effective strategies for spending or techniques for shopping.

Those are the mistakes that rob us of our spending power, and they can steal up to 20 percent of our incomes. Those of us most in need of help with our spending are least eager to follow traditional financial advice. Why? We enjoy spending, and we don't want to be told to stop!

The ideas in this book are for all of you, but most of all they should appeal to those of you who are reluctant to be told you must scrimp and save or make a budget. That's because this book offers a set of blueprints for constructing a style of competent, rewarding money management that may even involve spending more on yourself than you now do. In general, however, because you'll learn how to evaluate what you really want most, this book will show how you can get more for less money. You'll change from feeling powerless when it comes to money to being a successful spender.

I know you can, because I've done it. I learned how to look at why I spend. I learned how to share ideas with my husband about what we each want and enjoy and about the spending decisions we were making, as individuals and together.

Why did we take that hectic vacation two thousand miles from home? Why did I go ahead and buy that electric organ when my interest in playing it is so limited? Why did I spend so much eating out "for a treat" when the luxury I really craved was to hire someone to do the cleaning chores at home? "Why?" soon became the question I asked about every spending decision, large or small.

I learned to cut down on spending that doesn't buy any real pleasure or reward. I learned from mistakes my husband and I have made and a lot of the mistakes we've seen our friends and family making. I learned, too, to incorporate into my thinking the information I came across every day at work. For eight years I reported consumer news from researchers and other specialists at the University of California. I had at my fingertips the findings of experts in home economics, psychology, sociology, health, education and economics.

Here are some of these findings:

* Disastrous spending patterns can be understood in terms of transactional analysis. It is less often the selfish gratification impulse of the "child" in us than the unrealistic programming of the "parent" that triggers unwise spending decisions and leads families into debt.
* The use of leisure rather than ownership of possessions is the marker of status of the future, and there is a tendency throughout history for status symbols to filter downward through social classes.

* Elderly people who have been happiest throughout their lives are those who have an inner sense of direction rather than those who are easily influenced by outside factors.
* Advertisers play on our dreams or our fears and often promote silly and useless products.
* Twenty percent of the average consumer's income is wasted because of poor choices in food, clothing, household items, and similar purchases.

Everything I've learned about spending seems so obvious to me now. I've wondered many times why I needed so much time to learn how to put it to work.

What have I learned?

A successful spender isn't necessarily someone who spends less money. You don't have to give up your favorite splurges to be a wise spender, or use every tea bag twice and cut all your charge cards into small pieces. You don't have to scrimp and fidget, write down every penny you spend, or do anything you don't want to do. A surprising number of people discover that they *should* be spending more money on themselves, and that they actually *could* if they weren't spending their money in other, unprofitable ways.

This book should be especially useful to you in today's economic conditions. People who never used to have serious money worries are finding it is increasingly difficult just to come up with the money for routine expenditures. All of us are being squeezed by inflation. To some of us who grew up in the plentiful 1950s and 1960s this is a particular surprise. Many of us are now discovering that even a two-income household can't buy it all—or even very much. Those of us trying to plan a future style of living that will fit within a retirement income are hard-pressed to come up with projections that will balance income and outgo. It's time all of us learned how to stop spending in ways that don't buy any satisfaction.

If you become more competent at spending, you may not be able to own a fleet of exotic cars, buy all your clothes in expensive New York or Los Angeles shops, or take vacations to the French Riviera any time the whim strikes. The kind of financial success I am talking about involves freedom from financial hassles, with money in reserve; a standard of living that reflects your income rather than one that always seems to be falling behind; not having to live in circumstances in which you've used up all your options in advance and can't make any choices. You'll be in charge of your finances rather than the other way around.

Very likely the income and spending patterns you have now are neither providing you with riches nor leading you to poverty. You're probably somewhere in the middle. However, if there's any unsuccessful spending going on in your life, wouldn't you like to be able to rescue those dollars that are going in the wrong directions?

Before we start to do that, let's take a look at three common styles of spending that don't work well at all.

CHARLIE SPENDER

Here's the classic example of a guy who can't hold on to a dime. We've all known people like Charlie. In fact, some of us have been married to Charlies or have behaved just like him ourselves. Everybody thinks of Charlie as generous. In this case appearances are really deceptive, because Charlie is actually very selfish. He spends money to shore up his self-esteem.

Charlie works as a draftsman for an engineering firm. He's had the job for over ten years and has a good income, one that should be enough to support him and his family well. Charlie's a big, expansive man, with a smile for everyone. He'd give you the shirt off his back, but more than likely he'd have to use one of his credit cards to buy himself another shirt. He can't resist using his credit cards anyhow, and this is what makes Charlie's happy demeanor disappear when the bills come in at his house. Outgo is always more than income. Charlie is alternately morose and apologetic about his spending, and at the end of every conversation about money his wife ends up feeling like a quarrelsome nag.

She tells people that Charlie should have been a salesman like his father — with an expense account. His job doesn't require any selling or business camaraderie, but he acts as if it does.

Come payday he picks up the lunch tab for his buddies. Other days, on a whim, he buys a round of drinks after work or candy and trinkets for the secretaries. When he and his wife go out on a Saturday night, he's likely to invite everybody over for Sunday brunch.

What's more, Charlie has absolutely no sales resistance. The clerk at the local hardware store talked him into a "home food preparation center" with more attachments than a cordon bleu chef would want to use. An insurance man signed him up for an expensive policy to send both kids through college, even though Charlie's oldest is a seventh grader with little interest in her schoolwork. When the people in the office next door were getting together a group for an expensive weekend at a mountain resort, Charlie gladly signed up, too.

When they're trying to juggle the monthly payments, Charlie and his wife have talked about setting aside money for an orthodontist and for major repairs the car will soon need. From time to time Charlie talks about having enough money to go for a quiet fishing vacation. (I don't know whether he truly wants that vacation or not, but if he ever mentions it to the salesman at the hardware store he's likely to come home with a $200 fly rod.)

Charlie picked up his free-spending style from his father, for whom it apparently worked well enough. Charlie's father may also have been a compulsive spender, but he managed to indulge himself without demolishing the family finances. Charlie has copied his father's spending style, but it's not working in Charlie's circumstances. Why doesn't he catch on to what he's doing? Why can't he change?

I suspect that Charlie doesn't often examine his emotions. Moreover, it's probably only been in the last few years that his financial sins have really started to catch up with him. Credit-card spending takes some time to accumulate to genuinely painful levels. Expenses are increasing now that his kids are getting a little older. Finally, inflation has probably played the same dirty tricks on Charlie that it has on you and me.

I've said Charlie is a compulsive spender, so let's take time out to talk about that idea. What is a compulsion? According to

The American Heritage Dictionary it can mean "an irresistible impulse to act regardless of the rationality of the motivation, or an act or acts performed in response to such an impulse." I think most often of those things we do that bring unpleasant results but we do them anyway. This kind of behavior includes smoking, eating, or drinking too much, and also gambling, extramarital affairs, and nail-biting. It can also include all kinds of little things we do that go unnoticed by others, but when we do them we know we are working against ourselves.

Now let's take a look at another spending style that doesn't work very well.

SUSAN WAVERING

You may think Susan is a typical example of someone who is just starting out in life and hasn't settled down yet, but if you examine what she's doing you will see the problems in store for her. Susan is nineteen. She's been living away from home for over a year now. She works at a so-so office job, and talks from time to time about going to night school, looking for different work, or possibly planning for a vacation in Europe. She hasn't, however, taken any positive steps toward doing any of these things.

Susan has intermittent friendships with a lot of people but hasn't developed any lasting relationships with either males or females. She pounces briefly on new ideas and new friendships. Her enthusiasm is charming, but she wears people out with her quick changes of direction. In the last six months she's been on three diets, had a personal color analysis, stopped smoking several times, and, with a newfound friend, signed up for a correspondence course in interior design. Currently she is considering spending $50 to go with another friend to have her aura read, or spending a like amount to sign up in a self-defense class with yet another friend. She's having trouble deciding which, but in either event she'll cancel the correspondence course because she won't be able to make the remaining payments on it.

So far, Susan has been able to keep up with her charge accounts (at least the minimum payments) but she's written a few checks before she's actually had the money in the bank. She's behind on her telephone bill, mainly because of calls she made during her brief romance with a man who lived in another state. She often borrows small amounts to get through until payday, and she still sometimes eats and does her laundry at home or uses the family car.

Susan has little notion of economic realities. What's more, she's relying on others for just about all of her ideas of what she wants. Right now she's using up a lot of money in a pattern I call "zigzag spending" — using money for first one objective and then another, without really achieving any goal.

Many young people are like Susan. I think they are victims of their times. If Susan had grown up a generation earlier, she would have clearly understood that her mission in life was to find and marry a good provider. (I can remember the mother of one of my school friends telling her: "It's just as easy to fall in love with a professional man as with a gas station attendant.") However, while Susan was growing up that message wasn't being transmitted as clearly. Neither was the notion that young women ought to be serious about preparing to earn a good living. For quite some time, many of our young people have basked in a prosperous ambiance in which money-earning skills were devalued. These young people start out with a handicap.

NORM AND SHIRLEY PROPER

The Propers, by traditional standards a perfect example of wise money management, are spending just as unsuccessfully as Charlie or Susan. The Propers are thoroughly nice people, unselfish and responsible. Frugal, too. There isn't much they don't know about conserving money. Norm rotates the tires on his car, does all of his own yard work, and usually takes his lunch to the office. Shirley is faithful about getting shoes repaired, buys good clothes at end-of-season sales, and knows a number of distinguished ways to serve leftover chicken.

Norm has his own accounting business and Shirley works as a legal secretary. Their older son is married and has provided them with two grandchildren. Their daughter is away at college, and the younger son is in high school.

The Propers believe in the importance of keeping up appearances and plan carefully when it comes to spending money. They take particular pride in the gifts they send to their grandchildren. The daughter's college tuition is high, but they're pleased they are able to send her to an institution with a fine liberal arts tradition. They are in the process of paying Shirley's father's funeral expenses, and they maintain Norm's mother in an exclusive retirement home.

At the moment, the Propers are somewhat concerned because they've pledged two hundred dollars to the church building fund, and at the same time the younger boy has lost his part-time job—and there are a number of payments yet to be made on his new car. The bill collectors certainly aren't knocking on the Propers' door, but are Norm and Shirley managing their money as well as they think they are? Their lives are oriented to work and family, and seem colorless.

Actually, Norm and Shirley aren't drab people; they have their dreams. She is intensely interested in local politics and has considered running for city council. She has postponed turning this dream into reality until her job and home responsibilities are lighter. Norm has dreams of sailing. He subscribes to several boating magazines, and the plans for a splendid sailboat are stashed in his bottom desk drawer, along with newspaper articles about people who have built their own boats and gone on cruises to faraway places.

Each year when the Propers file their income tax return they review their financial situation. This year the story for them comes out the same as it has for quite some time: postpone the dreams and don't plan to cut down on working hours.

Norm and Shirley are victims of the standards established for their generation. Norm was brought up in the good-provider tradition, believing that if he did everything to earn money for Mom, apple pie, and the girl next door, he had the guarantee of a happy life. Shirley's high school counselor put into words the creed prevalent at the time: The only way for a woman to find happiness is to center her life around her husband and her children.

You can probably foresee what the Propers might do next. They will manage somehow to honor their pledge to the church fund and at the same time take care of those payments on their son's new car if he doesn't find another part-time job. The daughter at college can expect a lavish wedding, whether it's important to her or not, and those grandchildren will receive their share of largess.

The Propers are using dutiful spending, for which they were programmed and on which they can both agree, to avoid confronting some issues on which they likely won't agree. What if they stopped seeking out new financial responsibilities? Perhaps Shirley would quit her job, or cut back on her hours, and get involved in local politics. Perhaps Norm could get that sailboat and schedule a six-week cruise. He'd be looking to have his "first mate" at his side just when she's booked for a lengthy round of election work. What then?

The Propers may unconsciously fear finding out whether their relationship has the strength to keep them happily together while they negotiate a balance between their separate interests.

There's something else. Norm's only experience with boats has been as an armchair sailor. What if he discovers he has no taste for sleeping in a cramped bunk or eating the kind of meals that come from a three-weeks-at-sea galley? What if the endless routines of keeping everything shipshape just aren't his idea of fun? As for Shirley, she hasn't had any real experience with politics. She may quickly tire of having to remember everybody's name, sitting through dinners of creamed everything, being courteous to people she doesn't care for, or doing clerical chores not all that different from her work in the law office, but this time for free.

What if their individual dreams turn into dust and drudgery? They've lived with them so long and at such a comfortable distance. Will they have what it takes to rework the dreams into a reality they enjoy, or to abandon them and search for new ones?

∗ ∗ ∗

These are three examples of unsuccessful spending. Charlie spends incessantly in an effort to get something money can't buy — self-esteem. Susan's spending veers from this to that, and she never stops to confront either her lack of purpose or her lack of earning capacity to support a style of living she has come to expect. Norm and Shirley have learned how to acquire money, but they don't feel free about spending for themselves — or even about discovering what they want now that their earlier life goals have substantially been met.

Psychological and financial counselors across the country work with people like Charlie and Susan and the Propers every day. They know more about the pitfalls of their unsuccessful spending styles than we've talked about so far.

For instance, they know that Charlie's children will likely face some tough times unless they learn attitudes about money that don't spring from his. Charlie's daughter may have a special problem. She has already learned that Daddy just loves it when she catches him in an expansive mood and wheedles and flirts to get extra spending money.

What about Susan? Counselors have seen cases like hers end up in bankruptcy court. They have also seen young women like Susan jump into inappropriate marriages just to find a solution to their money problems. What's more, many young men and women with no sense of direction flee from the sense of economic insecurity and general purposelessness in their lives and wind up in the arms of recruiters from religious or other cults — cults structured to command every bit of their resources and time.

While the Propers will never turn up in bankruptcy court or join a cult, their style generates problems commonly seen by counselors. People like Norm and Shirley may subtly discourage their children from achieving financial independence. Sometimes nice people like the Propers spend their retirement years caught in a bitter, dismal trap of their own making. They may retreat into their separate fantasies about what they might have done, and they may harbor a surprising amount of repressed resentment toward the family members who "never appreciated what we did for them." If we stop to think about it, neither you nor I would want to spend the final decades of our lives in that frame of mind, not for any reason in the world.

In telling you about Charlie, Susan, and the Propers, I chose extreme examples and wound up with a gloomy picture. I did this to help you understand what successful spending is by showing you what it isn't. I'm not trying to imply that every person who fails to read this book is headed for bankruptcy, a religious cult, or a bitter old age. But I do want to make it clear that these are problematic spending patterns that can lead to trouble if they go unrecognized. The important point is this: You, and people you know who are like Charlie and Susan and the Propers, can *easily learn* the secrets of successful spending.

To help you get started, try thinking about some of the people you know and how happy they are in relation to how much money they have. There are a few people in this world who manage to lead remarkably satisfying lives with very little money. Many other people, with top earnings, have "misspent lives." They never seem satisfied and at times are downright frantic trying to meet their financial obligations.

What makes the difference?

Unsuccessful spenders make a lot of mistakes. They often don't really know what they want in life — today, next month, or next year. They seldom think about the choices they could make with the money available to them. Most don't take the time to think about why they spend as they do or how their spending attitudes and styles developed. Many, like Charlie, try to spend their way out of problems when the real solutions have to be achieved in another way. Some, like Susan, resist being in charge of their lives and put the responsibility for their spending decisions on their families, enticing advertisements, or luck. Finally, there are some like the Propers who don't spend enough money on themselves.

Successful spenders, by instinct or through experience and thoughtful analysis, have a very different approach to money. They are more aware of what they want out of life, or at least of what they genuinely enjoy. They seem to be especially skilled at finding the unadvertised specials in this world that will bring them real satisfaction. They understand the value of economic security without going overboard about it, and avoid the high costs of financial brinksmanship. They stay away from the kinds of spending that can be triggered by unhappiness and discord. They don't get caught in money traps, neither those set by people with something to sell, nor those that we are all capable of setting for ourselves. Finally, they have learned something of the tactics for making money decisions, and they know approaches to shopping that save both money and time.

2.

What in the World
Would You Like to Have?

I MAGINE YOURSELF in a situation in which you can have
anything you want. How about a perfect jewel of a sports car?
Maybe you dream of a vacation at a tropical resort with a waiter
at your beck and call. Maybe you'd like to have your own artist's
studio with nothing but the finest in materials and equipment.
Backpacking in Nepal? A Paris couturier to design each and
every item in your wardrobe? Your own stable of race horses?
Perhaps just one perfectly fitted pair of running shoes?

There are more things to buy, more ways to spend time and
money, than anyone in the world can possibly keep up with.
The availability of some of them is advertised to us every day.
Other kinds of things — often the ones that best express our
innermost preferences — aren't so well advertised. Nonetheless, they are available to us.

Suppose you have a wonderful source of income. Say there
are no more worries about utility bills, mortgage payments, car
payments, no loan installments due, groceries to buy, repair
bills, or similar responsibilities. Decide, if you want, that you are
rich enough to have anything. Have you ever thought about
what would make you happy? Just for now, think for yourself
only. Don't try to include what you think are the wishes of
anyone close to you. (Later in this book we'll talk about integrating your own spending plan with the plans and preferences of
other people in your life.)

Can you think of ten things you'd dream of having or doing? Think about it for a few moments if you want, and then go right ahead and make out your first list. Don't worry about setting things down according to priority. You will refine your thinking later. Just write down your wishes for now.

WHAT I DREAM OF

1.

2.

3.

4.

5.

6.

7.

8.

9.

10.

If you can't immediately think of ten things you would like to have or do with money, there's nothing at all unusual about you. I've asked a number of people to list ten things they would do with a splendid supply of money. Most put down a few ideas right away, but nearly all were fumbling by the time they reached seven or eight.

What kinds of things did people say they wanted? The lists would delight real estate and travel agents everywhere, as well as the folks who sell luxury cars. I analyzed the items on the lists people gave me, and here are the results.

Most frequently mentioned were consumer durables: cars, jewelry, cameras, pools, musical instruments, stereo equipment, boats, clothes. The second most frequently mentioned were altruistic wishes: "No child will ever go hungry" or "Peace and security worldwide." These responses say nice things about the people who made them. However, they are darn hard to buy. I suspect many people with these altruistic instincts would, if they indeed had the money, select good works that were more specific, closer to home, and capable of accomplishment.

Third most frequently mentioned on the lists was travel, although most people who chose it, made it the first item on their lists. Fourth most frequently mentioned was real estate, and after this, cultural and intellectual pursuits shared about equal frequency.

A typical list looked something like this:

WHAT I DREAM OF

---

1. Travel! Travel! Travel!

2. Financial security—pay off debts, invest for retirement.

3. Buy a Mercedes.

4. Contribute to worthy causes.

5. Buy a vacation house.

6. Jewelry—rubies, diamonds.

7. Get good stereo equipment.

8. Collect art seriously.

9. Endow a scholarship at my college.

10. A pool and a hot tub with a whirlpool pump.

People said interesting things about whether they would continue to work. Some emphasized they would quit their jobs. Perhaps others thought that stopping work went without saying, but such phrases as "invest for retirement" cropped up, and one person specified half-time work.

Some of the answers revealed insight into the true pleasures of financial security. One man, who loved to work in his carpentry shop, said he would buy a lot of new lumber instead of having to make do with used wood and scraps. One person — but only one — mentioned hiring a worker; he wanted to have someone complete the building of the patio he had started for his home. Only one person mentioned eating in a fine restaurant. That same person also said "stay home and relax" and "do a lot of window shopping and feel free to buy on impulse." These last answers are thoughtful ones and perhaps come closer to representing what people who have a lot of money might do.

What do the really moneyed people do?

Privacy, of course, is one of the privileges of the very wealthy. Our impressions of what moneyed people do come to us largely through the things they have done that they allow others to know about. These include the status symbols they choose to display.

In the nineteenth century, the wealthy had their own railway cars. Now they spend ninety thousand for a Rolls Royce, over a million for a private jet. The Onassis yacht, Christina, was valued at nearly six million, had a crew of sixty-five, and cost over a million a year to operate and maintain. The really wealthy customarily own residences here and abroad, and in both city and rural areas. Then they also spend money on their clothes, and jewelry, lavish entertainment and travel, fabulous restaurants and hotels.

Whether they do so privately or not, the wealthy invest a lot of time and money on mental and physical self-enchancement. They have hairdressers and masseurs, private doctors, dance instructors, and French tutors. They send their children to private schools to learn the habits and skills and attitudes that will forever mark them as "one of the tribe."

Whatever the wealthy choose to do, whether it's publicized or not, you can be certain they hire a great number of services performed for them. And you can be certain they have leisure.

If you think swiftly, this may be the point at which you say,

"Aha! Yes, the moneyed people have leisure, but I can have it, too." Leisure is one of the great unadvertised specials of this world.

Let's think about a concept I call the Money-Leisure Equation. Remember when you were still in school and living with your parents? If you are like a great number of us, you alternated between having a part-time job and not working. If you were working, you had money but little time in which to spend it. Otherwise you had the time but not a nickel in your jeans. You may have put this into words: When I've got money, I don't have any time to spend it; when I've got time, I don't have any money.

That's the Money-Leisure Equation. For those of ordinary means, there's always a tradeoff between money and leisure. Most of us learned this as we approached adulthood. But when we became more and more involved in meeting our everyday responsibilities, this piece of wisdom seemed to slip away. When we have more money most of us consider buying more things. We forget that we have an option for leisure.

Time to do things is the number-one divider that separates the "idle rich" from the "working class." What's more, the use of leisure rather than the ownership of possessions is likely to become more and more important for all the income groups between rich and poor. It is a powerful mark of status.

Today an upwardly mobile two-income household often can afford a Porsche, a good stereo, cashmere sweaters, and the like. This means the folks who can pay for the same things with just one income will likely seek other ways to express their higher status. They will use their relatively abundant leisure to establish this distinction. They may own a pair of Afghan hounds, perfectly trained and groomed. They may acquire skill at Cantonese cooking, contract bridge, or water polo. Whatever the distinction is, you can bet your bottom dollar it will be something no one can buy on the installment plan, and it will require leisure.

Ask yourself if you really want some of the "things" you've been saying you want. If you enjoy them for their intrinsic qualities, that's fine. However, you may want to rethink your decisions, if the things you want are to serve as a mark of your status in this economic world.

You can "keep up with the Jones'," if that's what brings you satisfaction or meets some particular need. You can also find other ways to enhance your life, such as hiring someone to do the housecleaning or the yard work.

If you had plenty of time and a modicum of money, what would you do? Here are a few ideas to help you get your own list started

* Spend time with someone you love.
* Take a walk before breakfast if you feel like it.
* Read as much as you want to.
* Take up painting, or guitar, or woodcarving.
* Start a physical fitness program.
* Join an amateur drama group.
* Work to develop a small but well-coordinated wardrobe, with everything in it a perfect fit.
* Be a community leader.
* Get a beautiful suntan.
* Learn a lot about something—local history, film making, motorcycles, antique clocks.
* Have a perfect manicure and pedicure.
* Write your family history.
* Become skilled in another language.
* Study calligraphy.

Later I am going to ask you to list the uses of leisure that interest you the most. For now, you may want to mark ideas from this list that you like, or you may want to keep in mind a few of your own.

We have considered what the average person thinks of when it comes to a dream list of what to do with money. We've looked at a few of the things that the moneyed people do. We've talked about the Money-Leisure Equation and how the uses of leisure can be marks of status. Finally, I've asked you to think a little about what you would like to do with leisure.

Now it's time to do some serious exploration of the options you have. You've learned that most people who haven't had a chance to think about their spending options make up lists of buyable "things" along with some general altruistic wishes and some expressions of concern about financial security. You also know that most of these people don't think of the hiring of services and all the enjoyable pursuits that require leisure. Now that you have had a chance to develop some more thoughtful ideas about what you would do with money, you may want to start thinking about what you would like to do with leisure.

Let's take an analytical approach, by using a system of lists that takes everything into consideration. Suppose now that you're no longer working with an unlimited source of money. Think instead in terms of an excellent money supply and in terms of ambitious-but-possible. Your dream list should have served a useful purpose, however. "I think it was very important to have an element of fantasy at the start of the process," one of my friends told me. "People should dream for a while about what can be done with unlimited money. This is a fantasy, but fantasy is how people climb mountains — get big things done."

Revise your list of objectives, yes, but don't completely toss out all those wonderful things. Look for the key elements in each dream and for ways to scale these down into something achievable.

Your analytical approach, your lists of attainable objectives that take everything into consideration, will be in four categories: Security, Caring for Others, Buyables, and Leisure.

Here are some guidelines to help you include everything you want, and make sure you've got each of your wishes in the correct category.

Category One: Security. Security involves anything related to how you earn a living (provisions for earning more, working less, or doing something more interesting) how you expect to insulate yourself from financial hardship, how you're going to provide financial help for anyone to whom you feel obligated, and how you eventually plan to retire.

If you are like many of the people I've asked to fill out lists, you will have to separate your objectives from the means to achieve these objectives.

Here are some examples of Security objectives:

* Prepare to get into a different and more interesting career.
* Quit working before I'm fifty!
* Help children go to school/get established.
* (For full-time homemakers) Set up a means to have more help with household responsibilities.
* Care for elderly relatives.
* Have retirement income adequate for monthly expenses and some travel.
* Own a paid-for house with a place to garden when I retire.

Here are some examples of means to achieve those Security objectives:

* Pay off debts.
* Cut down expenses.
* Own a good stock portfolio.
* Build up savings account.
* Buy rental property.
* Invest in gold.

When you get to writing the Security part of the list, you will have a space to list both your objectives and the means to achieve those objectives. Whatever your circumstances and whatever your objectives, you should at the very least make sure your overall earning and spending patterns leave you with some money to set aside for emergencies, special purposes, and future needs.

Another point to remember. If you feel obliged to help someone in the family who is ill or elderly, be sure you talk over your plan of action. That aunt you expected to set up in a senior citizens' apartment in your city may surprise you with plans of her own to live on a communal farm in Oregon or a houseboat in Florida!

Category Two: Caring for Others. You should not put down here things you feel *obligated* to do. This list is for *voluntary* wishes, the altruistic things you'd like to do. Many of the items will be your own individual wishes. Others you may have developed jointly with your family, such as support for your church,

Little League, or other community activities. Do you want to form a group to raise money for a local museum? Do you want to provide for a specific set of the world's needy children or lonely people? Do you support a service club, the Sierra Club, League of Women Voters, or the local "Y"? Do you want to carry out any good works on a person-to-person level? Help friends or relatives to whom you're *not* obligated? Think of time or services you want to donate as well as money. Do you want to change any of your present altruistic activities to something in which you have a more specialized talent or just to get some variety?

Category Three: Buyables. You may want to use more space than is provided on the list. This category includes those well-advertised things you've likely wanted all along. You should also include whatever real estate you would like for residence, vacation, or variety. (But real estate *investment* belongs in Category One, Security.) Add all the vacation and travel resorts, restaurants, and expensive entertainment in theaters, cabarets, and the like. Be sure you include what you want in the way of jewelry, clothes, cars, stereos, sports equipment, antiques and collectibles, expensive pets, pools, musical instruments, works of art, furniture, fine linens, expensive tools — whatever you have a hankering for that can be found in a catalogue or store or that you've seen advertised anywhere.

This is the place where you'll have to make a thoughtful transition from your dream list to your more realistic list. As you do this, however, I hope you can keep the essence of some of those wonderful dream wishes you wrote down — wishes that may have been too expensive for ordinary mortals. Don't toss out even the most extravagant ideas without some careful thought. You may be able to capture an achievable piece of the action.

On the other hand, you may have been mistaken about what you wanted. Sometimes when you try to discover the essence of what's desirable about an item from your dream list, you may draw a complete blank. If you can't find an achievable portion on which your thoughts linger with delight, perhaps you should reconsider the dream. Sometimes when you haven't thought matters through, you go along with conventional ideas about what you are supposed to want even if you would derive scant enjoyment from it if you actually owned it.

Category Four: Leisure. This, in case you haven't guessed, is my favorite. This is the category that includes all of the world's unadvertised specials. It's also the one in which you can make best use of your creativity and imagination. Include on this list services in and around your home that could provide you with more free time. Put down classes and other instruction in recreational skills, self-improvement, intellectual pursuits and the like, including college if you plan to attend for the joy of learning rather than to enhance your wage-earning potential.

Add personal physical enhancement beyond routine barber and beauty shop care. (This could run into big money, if you want cosmetic surgery!) Add any visits you would like to make to see relatives or friends if these involve substantial travel costs or amounts of time. Put down the local bookstore, art supply house, sports shop, camera shop, or any other place you would spend money to enhance your recreation or hobbies.

Don't needlessly discard any dream; look instead for ways to sort out an achievable piece of it. If you think you'll never have the chance to learn to play a full-scale theater organ, there may be a smaller version in a church in your neighborhood on which you could practice. If you're too old to try to aim for the Olympics, that doesn't mean you're restricted to being an armchair athlete. However, you may also have simply accepted a standardized dream if you discover you can't scale down your wishes. It could be that your mother has you convinced you've always wanted a high-style wardrobe, or you've dreamed of mountain climbing because of the image associated with this sport rather than because of any real love for what's involved.

Now you are about to start a thorough and thoughtful job of making your lists. Don't worry if you're beginning to feel that you're being led into never-never land, that there's no purpose to be served by making up lists of things you can't afford right now. Consider the principles of management by objectives. You know you can't evaluate your success unless you know what you are trying to accomplish. The purpose of making these lists is to help you start establishing those objectives. Have faith! You'll

probably change your objectives somewhat as the years go by
— and besides, you've got the rest of your life to achieve your
objectives.

Here are forms you can use for your lists. Don't worry if you
don't fill up the spaces or have to use a second sheet of paper.
Everyone is different. You can put your copies of these lists into
a notebook which I suggest you start.

CATEGORIZED LIST OF OBJECTIVES

CATEGORY ONE: SECURITY

(Objectives—employment, retirement, obligations.)

1.

2.

3.

4.

5.

6.

7.

8.

9.

10.

(Means to achieve objectives—debt reduction, investments, rentals, etc.)

1.

2.

3.

4.

5.

6.

7.

8.

9.

10.

CATEGORY TWO: CARING FOR OTHERS

(Voluntary altruistic wishes, including church, college or personal charity.)

1.

2.

3.

4.

5.

6.

7.

8.

9.

10.

CATEGORY THREE: BUYABLES

(Consumer durables, real estate, vacations—just about everything that is advertised for sale.)

1.

2.

3.

4.

5.

6.

7.

8.

9.

10.

11.

12.

13.

14.

15.

16.

17.

18.

19.

20.

CATEGORY FOUR: LEISURE
(Services to buy, things to learn for fun, hobbies, time for people.)

1.

2.

3.

4.

5.

6.

7.

8.

9.

10.

11.

12.

13.

14.

15.

Obviously, you aren't going to achieve all the objectives you've put down here, at least not soon. Nonetheless, these lists have given you a start at defining and sorting out your own truest wishes. You've got it down in writing, all those things you want out of life. If you like, go back and mark one or two items in each category that are particularly important to you.

You will be using these lists to make schedules for achieving objectives you select from them. You'll likely share the lists with others in your life and compare notes on fondest dreams. Don't forget to keep these lists, along with all of the other lists and worksheets I'll ask you to do in this book.

3.

Your Choices
in a Real World

I HOPE YOUR HEAD is still filled with images of all the things you want, because now it's time to talk about some of the how-to's of deciding — the thoughts that you should have before you make any choices.

For the purpose of talking about successful spending I have my own definitions of options and choices. *Options* are unlimited. They are all of those wonderful things you might have. *Choices* are limited. They are the decisions you will make. As a successful spender you must make your choices within the limits of your resources.

Whether you plan them or not, you make spending choices throughout your lifetime. These choices should, for the most part, be well thought out. I'm not suggesting that anyone should try to plan every instant and every penny in life. Impulse spending can be delightfully rewarding. However, your spending decisions should usually be thoughtful, and they should be your own. Seldom should they be decisions by default, not if you are to get your money's worth.

Later on we'll talk about various factors that affect your spending choices as an individual. Right now let's take a look at the influences that increase your potential for decision by default. It's important to remember that there are people in this world who are out to acquire money by selling things to you. It may sound paranoid, but those people are plotting to get your money! This is so simple and straightforward most of us hardly think about it.

The situation is described in almost any basic economics text. I'll quote from a book by Leland Gordon and Stewart Lee, *Economics for Consumers.*

"Traditional economic analysis begins with one basic fact of life: the insatiability of human wants. It is presumed that the desires of consumers for goods and services are capable of indefinite expansion. Most economists accept this as a basic fact so obvious that it requires no demonstration."

The authors later say: "In a free-enterprise economy, producers of goods and services produce the things they expect will yield the greatest profit. The welfare of consumers is secondary." They go on to explain that much will be produced that has no value to the consumer's well-being, or has a negative value. You might make your own translation: producers of goods and services aren't thinking of your welfare at all!

So there it is, right out in the open.

There's a commercial world full of people operating on the premise that they can sell you something whether it is wise for you to buy it or not. They'd like to try for all of your available money, and they'll okay your credit almost every time. You can't blame them. However, you can wonder who is in charge of your life if they get your money before you've made your own best decision about what to do with it.

You don't have to buy everything all those folks are selling. Who *is* in charge of your life? If you are to make the best use of your money, you should be in charge.

There is a concept psychologists call "locus of control." This is an awkward phrase, but it has a meaning that is easy to understand. It refers to the feeling people have about whether or not they are in control of their lives. If your locus of control is within yourself, you tend to feel in charge of your destiny. At least you feel in charge of how you respond to events in your life, even if you can't plan or control everything that happens to you. You think ahead to what might be coming and consider alternative ways to cope with it. You think about how you would like things to be for yourself and about various ways to go after those things you want.

What if your locus of control is elsewhere? You may often feel rather buffeted by circumstances, never knowing where the next push or shove is coming from. You may hope for a few good breaks from the powers-that-be, Lady Luck, or whatever outside influences you think have some control over what happens to you. You may tend to feel that someone else in the family should be making the decisions.

If you want to make use of your money wisely, you will have to work toward making the most of that sense of control within yourself. Sometimes this isn't easy. A decision you make for yourself is one you have to take responsibility for. Nonetheless, you will be far better off in the long run if you build the habit of making your own choices from the options available to you.

Life's happiest people feel in control of their actions. Professor Joseph Kuypers, a researcher at the University of California's Institute for Human Development at Berkeley, studied a number of people in their late sixties in relation to whether or not they felt in charge of their lives. His research was an attempt to learn who succeeds in the lifelong pursuit of happiness. Slightly more than half the people he studied did feel they were in charge of their lives; slightly less than half did not feel that this was so.

People who feel in control of their lives "are able to take action that achieves greater self-enhancement," Kuypers said when I interviewed him about his research. "They believe in their own ability to shape and influence what happens to them and are more adaptable. They are more in touch with the flow between past, present and future; they anticipate and prepare for events, and they choose more appropriate responses and stand up less fearfully to change." Kuypers said he found that people who do not feel in charge of their lives tend to cope less well, and are "more given to self-doubt, passivity, and dependence."

If you have tended to be a believer in fate, or won't make a move without consulting your daily horoscope, maybe it's time you start acting upon the idea that it is you who has the captainship of your life.

For his research Kuypers categorized his subjects as either believing or not believing that they could control their own destiny. I think people may operate either one way or the other depending on circumstance. But we are all capable of thinking about the situation in which we find ourselves, the probable source of control for our decisions in these circumstances, and whether we would benefit from lessening our dependence on outside influences.

To begin with, listen to your thoughts about purchases you are making. Watch out if you find yourself thinking thoughts like these:

* I don't want it all that much, but everybody has one.
* I really ought to buy it because the salesperson has been so nice, or has taken so much time with me.
* I guess I can afford it because they okayed my credit.

If these kinds of thoughts have been part of your style, you'd best start considering who is in charge of your life.

There are still other factors that can influence your ability to be a successful spender. We have all been programmed in specific ways about spending money, based on whether we are male or female, how old we are, and the money attitudes with which we grew up.

Let's consider first the differences in programming between males and females. Many men start out with a particular handicap here, because their traditional upbringing doesn't allow them to feel comfortable thinking about their emotions. Feelings of elation, anger, pride, jealousy, accomplishment, or inferiority are tied up with how we all spend money. Men, however, tend to suppress awareness of their feelings. This was true in the case of Charlie Spender.

Men are in luck when it comes to mechanical and tool-related problems around the house or in the car. They've often been brought up to cope with simple repairs themselves. (Women can learn too of course, as so many nowadays are.)

Men are often out of luck when it comes to housekeeping. They feel less free than women about operating outside of sex-role stereotypes. Keeping things neat, tended, and sorted out is often thought of as sissy — women's work. But a lot of money is likely to go down the drain when men buy something they already have on hand but can't locate or have forgotten, or when they step on something and break it because it was lost in the clutter, or neglect something until it's no longer suitable for use.

Men are particularly disadvantaged by their programming to spend money to demonstrate their masculinity. Some will spend to try to impress a pretty woman, the other guys, or their families. By now, a lot has been said about the hazards of the risk-taking macho ideal of a man who drives fast, drinks hard, and spends big. However, the men most in need of rescue from this syndrome seem the least inclined to listen to any analysis of their psyche.

How are women disadvantaged? Nearly all women have their own programming when it comes to how they look. A woman who carefully weighs a ten-cent difference in the purchase of something at the supermarket will without hesitation decide to embark on an expensive hair-coloring job that costs a lot of money every month to maintain. Men often say women are vain, but traditional female vanity has a practical basis. This so-called vanity is based on the still more or less valid precept that a woman has to be good-looking to get along well in this world. Women are vulnerable to the merchandisers of expensive cosmetics, high-fashion clothes, and a host of other products that won't necessarily make any genuine improvement in their looks.

Women face another hazard because they have been traditionally schooled to be passive when it comes to major financial planning and decision making. That same lady who can recite supermarket prices of myriad items with incredible accuracy may turn into putty when it comes to selecting investments or negotiating with a car salesman. The "Whatever you say, Dear," syndrome controls her as she lets her husband handle the whole thing or blindly follows the advice of the nearest available male.

Even today we're haunted by traditional images of what it means to be male or female. When it comes to money, always be aware of the possibility that sex-stereotyping is influencing what you are doing. Flex as many muscles or wear as many ruffles as you please, but don't let such things interfere with your capacity to make sound spending decisions.

There's another major influence on our patterns of spending. It's how old we are, or, more specifically, what set of ideas we grew up with. As you may remember, I said that Susan Wavering, and also the Propers, were victims of their times. Let me explain what I meant by telling you some of the conclusions we can draw if we know a person's generation.

If you came of age before 1950, chances are your outlook is traditionalist. Your spending style, in greater or lesser degree, may resemble the Propers. You are likely to value economic security, stability, and quite a number of material things. You believe in the value of work and social order. You are a good team player. You may spend more on others than you would on yourself, and you tend to expect that the people on whom you spend money will take care of you, too. You may feel ill at ease with unstructured leisure time.

If you came of age more recently, your set of values is more self- and process-oriented. You probably value work for its self-fulfillment potential, and you are far likelier to value experiences more than things. You are open to change and experiment, and you rely less on established concepts of social order than on concepts of ability and equality. However, you are less likely to be a team player and more likely to have achieved economic independence with some slowness. As a spender you may have experienced some of the purposelessness that characterized Susan Wavering, and you are far more likely to overuse credit than the traditional generation that preceded you.

I don't think any of us can or should undo all of the assumptions basic to the style of life with which we grew up. Many of these ideas and ideals are valuable. However, we can and should become more certain about who we are and how this may influence our spending outlook — and we can apply the same insights to those whom we love and live with.

Your gender and your age will certainly affect your spending attitudes, but family attitudes toward money (the attitudes you soaked up during childhood) probably have the most influence. Charlie Spender's wife recognized the roots of his spending patterns in his father's style. Are you aware of how many of your spending decisions are determined by your childhood programming? Here are some points to ponder.

Did your family help you learn how to handle money decisions with reason? Could you acquire money on a regular basis so you could count on making plans for what to do with it, or did it come sporadically at the whim of others? Did you get the idea you were supposed to spend it all as soon as you got it or save some? How much encouragement or reward did you get to save? Did you discover that gifts often came with strings attached, such as spending money that was partly for the church collection or school lunches? Did you learn never to save because your older sibling always swiped your hoard?

How did your parents interact when it came to money? Did your father often use a big expenditure to apologize to your mother? Were costly gifts the principal means of expressing love at important holidays? Were the women in your family expected to spend money in frivolous ways to enhance everyday living while the men were expected to make major expenditures related to the course of everyone's life? Did either parent control the other by doling out money? Did either express anger by spending or withholding money?

What general attitudes did you pick up? Did you hear people being praised for being thrifty or condemned for being stingy? Were the men you heard your family talk about admired for being quick about reaching for their wallets? Was your mother kept in the dark about family finances? Were you usually aware of whether it was just before or just after payday in terms of food, spending money, and the general nature of what was happening around the house? Did you grow up in an atmosphere of never-enough or always-plenty? Are you still following practices dictated by those circumstances even if your current situation is different?

Once you've begun to examine the money attitudes you were brought up with, you will discover some ways these attitudes have been shaping your spending decisions or the decisions of people close to you.

You may be interested in looking at the differences between

you and any brothers and sisters you have. Similar circumstances can produce a surprising variety of results. Resist the temptation to become your brother's keeper and offer a lot of free advice, but surely you should look at your siblings' spending attitudes to gain a better understanding of your own.

There is a very interesting method for discovering the set of ideas that control your behavior and looking at whether these ideas are rational or not. This method was explained to me by a man who worked for the U.S. State Department. He taught a course about differences in cultures in a training institute for those employees soon to be sent to foreign countries.

"Whenever I want to find out about what is at the root of a practice," he said, "I start asking why something is done. I will usually be given a somewhat rational explanation at first. With each answer, I continue to ask why. When people stop giving reasonable answers and start shouting 'Just because!' I know I am beginning to discover something."

You may not want to take quite this approach, but consider the usefulness of asking why on any spending decision that seems to be covered by some sort of automatic decision-making system. Of course, you do have to pay for that hamburger before you leave the restaurant, and you do have to pay the rent or the mortgage. But there are plenty of other spending decisions that you can think about.

Here's one example. A couple I know, who live in the cool Northwest, were considering buying a new car. They both wanted an economy model, but the husband kept saying they must have a car with an engine large enough to easily support an air conditioner. In fact, he insisted their car should be equipped with air conditioning. Why? His puzzled wife kept asking the question. Finally, he responded, almost in anger, "Well, anybody who is anybody has a car with air conditioning, and that's that!" He might as well have shouted, "Just because!" He wasn't really thinking about it, but preconceived and rigid notions were governing how he was going to spend his money. In that particular situation, those notions were going to override any practical considerations. "Just because!" thinking can cost a lot of money.

So far in this chapter we've talked about patterns that may affect your spending choices and the advantages you can enjoy by taking charge of your own decision making. We've talked about the influences of gender, generation, and family attitudes on your ability to make good spending decisions.

Consider now the decisions your're making to maintain your standard of living. How difficult is it to cut down on expenses that you have considered necessary? How can you have more choices? You may already have developed some of your own ideas about this, but home economics experts say we could cut down by about twenty percent without making any basic changes in our lifestyle.

That's right. Twenty percent, and this figure comes from home economists at the University of California, who say that this kind of waste comes from lack of knowledge and poor decisions in food, clothing, and purchases of other things for the home.

They say that half the money spent for clothing and textiles goes for things not used or not worn out because of poor choices in color, design, or fit. On average, they say, ten percent of a family's budget goes for clothing. As to food, twenty percent more than is necessary is often spent. Food costs may represent as little as six percent of the family budget in high income groups, but range up to half among poor people. Similar losses in spending power come from poor choices in home furnishings, appliances, and housing. Even higher losses can occur when shopping decisions are left to inexperienced and untrained teenagers or when a family experiences marital discord or some other unhappy circumstance.

You can't, of course, have a home economist at your elbow every time you go to the store. However, you can give careful attention to even the small choices without being penny wise and pound foolish, and wind up maintaining your lifestyle — but not supporting careless mistakes as well.

In making larger choices you have an even greater potential for savings. This is especially true when it comes to adjusting your lifestyle so that you can take advantage of choices that save money over time. You can free large amounts of money to spend as you please by the choices that you make about how much you'll invest in housing, how far you plan to live from work, whether your wardrobe will be fashion-plate or utility, and so forth. You can also select among these major choices to have the one you value most.

Take just one decision: commuting to work. Here are figures from the Federal Highway Administration. If you drive a standard-size car for a distance of twenty miles to your job, your annual costs for owning and operating the vehicle just for commuting would be $1,857 (in 1979). You could reduce both ownership and operating costs if you opted instead to drive a subcompact and live only ten miles from work. Your annual costs would then be $726. Even if living nearer your job increased your housing costs, I doubt if the difference would be that much. What's more, if you chose to stop being a "lone ranger," when you drive to work, you could save even more. If you shared a ride in a small car with just one other partner your annual costs would go down to $398. The difference between the twenty-mile solo commute in a standard car and the ten-mile commute in a smaller car with one other person is $1,459. That comes — in full-sized after-tax dollars — to just over $120 a month. What interesting things could you do with that amount of money?

You will have a chance to work out a number of your short- and long-range lifestyle choices in later chapters. But now it's time to talk about how to take an inventory of your current spending and begin to develop a framework on which you can start building your spending success.

4.

Taking Inventory of Your Spending

M OST OF US have tried at one time or another to take a closer look at what we spend. It's not always easy.

Let me tell you about someone I talked with while I was putting together the ideas for this book. He's a nice man, quite intelligent, with a nearly grown family. Some gray hair at his temples and crinkle lines around his eyes give him a look of wisdom, but I don't think he's been very wise about how he spends money. He's complained to me about his financial worries from time to time, and in one particular conversation he said that he never knew where his money went.

This was one area in which I felt I could offer some help. I'm proud of the system I've worked out over the years for keeping track of my spending, or at least for getting enough information to measure how I'm doing. I reassured my friend and told him he should try my no-hassle system. All he had to do, I told him, was use his checking account to keep track of where his money went. He expressed some doubts. Then he admitted that he didn't always fill in his check stubs.

"You don't even need to do that," I told him. "You can work from your cancelled checks."

This was when he really surprised me.

"I never look at my cancelled checks," he said. "I just don't want to look at anything in my bank statement!"

I didn't see any purpose in finishing my explanation. We haven't talked since about his money problems, but I've thought many times about what he said. Very few of us have such an extreme attitude, but most of us do some sidestepping and procrastinating when it comes to finding out where all those dollars go. We all suffer to some degree from what I call Fear of Budgeting.

Although most of us don't experience Fear of Budgeting as severely as my friend, this fear is a common one. It's also rather complicated. There are many reasons why we avoid keeping track of what we spend. If we know what these reasons are, we'll be better able to cope with them and to get on with the relatively easy process of tracking our expenditures.

Some of the elements in Fear of Budgeting are:

* Fear that our secrets, even the ones we've kept from ourselves, will be revealed.
* Fear that we will fail and will have to add this failure to all the plans to attempt diets, physical fitness programs, and other self-disciplinary measures we've hidden away in a bottom drawer or in the back of our minds.
* Fear that we will have to stop spending. We've managed somehow to support a host of minor indulgences, and maybe now we'll have to be logical and not enjoy them anymore.

With my budgeting system, you don't need to be afraid for any of these reasons. You can have as much privacy as you like. You're not going to fail. What's more, the only thing you are going to give up is the kind of spending that doesn't buy you much satisfaction. Examining these reasons why people fear budgeting will help you conquer any fears you may have.

First is the idea that you won't be able to keep secrets or have enough privacy. Most of us sequester money for private purposes. If you like, you can imagine your own awful headlines:

WOMAN, OTHERWISE NORMAL,
SPENDS $13 MONTHLY ON BUBBLE GUM

LOCAL BUSINESSMAN ADMITS
OWNING 40 PAIRS OF SOCKS

These are silly, but a little silliness can help put our fears in perspective. No one is entirely logical, and none of us wants certain things made public. Your secrets? Maybe you're stashing something like sailboat plans or hiding money for some private purpose. Maybe you don't want yourself to know how much is going out for nicotine, or alcohol, or whatever your compulsion is. Whether our aims are innocent or not, whether our spending is large or small, we all like a little financial elbow room.

Nonetheless you can and should overcome any fears you have of knowing how you spend. My approach to budgeting won't require you to examine details any more closely than you want to. The emphasis is on what you want, not on what you shouldn't do. If you are spending money on things that aren't good for you, you won't cut back much on this spending anyhow unless you begin to want something else more — and believe you will be able to have it.

So much for the fear of losing privacy. Next is fear of failure. Many people don't want to budget because they don't want to add to their collection of small failures. We've all experienced the Great Expectations/Immediate Flop routine.

Here's what I'm talking about. First, you start with an unrealistic goal, often accepted from an outside source. You've read an article in the Sunday paper and perhaps made a promise to someone to do something about it. You enjoy a brief period of basking in the anticipation of your wonderful behavior. You're going to start getting up at 5:30 A.M. and do all those exercises. You're going to follow that diet to the letter, and stick to 1140 calories a day until you lose seventeen pounds. You're going to smash a two-pack-a-day habit cold turkey.

You're familiar with what happens next. Just once you reset the alarm and take a little extra snooze, or you accept a doughnut someone offers, or light up just one cigarette — and what a relief! You've achieved the failure. You can abandon the whole thing and go back to your usual ways.

The Great Expectations/Immediate Flop routine applies to keeping track of money, too. People buy those accountant's pads of wide yellow paper. Or they set up a complicated set of envelopes to reserve money for each kind of expense. The accounting pads and the envelopes have worked well for some people, but you don't need such complex systems. Most of all you don't need a set of expectations that are doomed to failure. Don't accept the idea that if you keep track of money you are immediately going to stop eating out, or spending money for clothes or recreation. You won't have to act like a world champion miser. You know that if you set yourself up for the Great Expectations/Immediate Flop routine, the first time you head for McDonald's or decide to take in a movie you're likely to drop the whole enterprise and hide it in some sort of mental bottom drawer. Keep in mind that you're not setting out to be perfect but just to keep a record of your spending.

The third element in Fear of Budgeting is the idea that spending will have to stop. Some of this fear can be alleviated just by avoiding the Great Expectations/Immediate Flop routine. Nonetheless, this is a tough one to resolve especially if you now spend more than you earn or if your current spending habits are in conflict with a desire to save money.

I can offer two helpful ideas. The first is that you try separating the pleasure you get from whatever you spend money for from the pleasure you get from the actual transaction. We all enjoy some of the things associated with buying. It's gratifying to have a salesperson pay attention to us. There is a pleasure in being the person who can plunk money down or whip out a credit card. Perhaps sometimes you get a genuine benefit from that small gratification. However, you should be aware of what you are doing. The pleasure of being a big spender is short-lived and costly.

Here's the second idea. Whatever you spend money for will force you to give up something else. You can only spend the money once. When you are tempted to spend it for something you don't need or aren't truly sure you want, keep in mind that this purchase displaces something that could be more important to you. It may help to look the salesperson in the eye and think, "This is the guy who's trying to take my ski boots away from me," or "This is the so-and-so who is going to make me work overtime next month."

The third obstacle to budgeting, the fear that you will have to stop spending, will always be there. In order to get on with the business of keeping track of your spending, you may simply have to ignore it. Keep remembering that your goal is only to record your spending, not to make drastic changes.

Here's one final suggestion. Make a sign in your imagination. Think of it as posted on the inside of your forehead. You can always see it with your mind's eye. The sign says:

W H A T   I   W A N T   I S   O K A Y.

So now we're ready to get on with my accounting system. How much money are you spending? How do you spend it? How on earth are you going to find out? The easiest way, as I told my friend, is to use your monthly bank account statement. Here's how this no-hassle, no-fail system works.

Start when you get your bank statement. I find it's easier to work from the middle of one month to the middle of the next, because that's more or less how my bank statement is set up. However, you can arrange your month any way you want. All you will have to do is make two lists from the information in your bank statement and your cancelled checks. One list will be the amount of cash you have spent. The other list will include everything you've paid by check.

Your objective will be to get four basic totals: cash spent for the month, installment payments, interest on installment payments, and installment debt still due. There are many ways to keep accounts, but these totals will provide enough information so that you can mark progress toward the goals you set for yourself.

Here's my worksheet for your no-hassle audit, which you can add to your notebook.

MONTHLY AUDIT Time period: _____

CASH	NOT CASH
Total cash _____	Total installments _____
	Total interest _____
	Total debt still due _____

Your first task is to list Cash spending. Go through your checks and put down any you wrote for cash, plus any you wrote at the grocery store (whether you spent all the money for groceries or not). Got anything you'd care to label ESP? That stands for Expenditure Some Place, and it's a great privacy keeper. Your ESPs will be here, assuming you paid cash. What else? Put down any amount you deducted in cash from your paycheck when you deposited it. Did you spend any money that did not go through your checking account, such as money you received in cash for work you've done or loans repaid to you? Put that into the Cash listing. Add money that came as a gift.

Now to your second task, the Not-Cash column. List everything you paid by check except those checks written at the grocery store or elsewhere for cash. Your Not-Cash column will include the rent or mortgage payment, loan installments, credit card payments, utility and telephone bills, insurance bills, payments to department stores, doctor and dentist bills, and the like. If you paid rent or some other such bill in cash, fudge a bit and put this on the Not-Cash side.

You won't need to add up all of your expenses on the Not-Cash side of your worksheet, only some of them. First, circle all of your loan, credit card, or department store installments. Do this for any loan other than your mortgage installment. Then add these up. Write the total at the bottom of your Not-Cash column. Now go back through the loan statements (other than your mortgage) and add up the interest or service charges. Put this total down, too, right under the loan installment total. Finally go through the statements again, to determine the installment debt not yet paid.

You have just completed your first monthly no-hassle audit.

You can add some frills and extras to your audit system if you're feeling ambitious. If long-distance phone calls are often your financial undoing, you may want to start a month-to-month phone tally. You may want to group together the items you paid by check to have an idea of how much is going out in certain other categories. These may include clothing, transportation, major acquisitions for your household — whatever you've decided you especially want to monitor. You don't have to do anything mentioned in this paragraph. These ideas are strictly optional.

Another option is available to you. If you want, you can file all of the various receipts and other pieces of paper related to money in the bank envelope along with your cancelled checks. I find this very useful as a means of locating something a few months later. Also, this is the way I keep money records in anticipation of income tax time.

Frills and extras aside, what have you accomplished with your Monthly Audit? You've got four totals. These totals will serve as checkpoints to measure your successful spending progress when you do audits in future months.

I'm assuming that you are like most of us. You would like to cut down on your debts. You'd probably also like to cut down a little on the pocket money you spend. As you keep track of your totals each month you should feel like you're ahead of the game if you see the amounts get smaller each time. You should get particular satisfaction in seeing the amount you pay for installment interest decline. There is real pleasure in winning this numbers game. But what do you get for a prize if you're the winner? You'll have the money to spend for the things you want most.

What do you want to do with your money right now or in the very near future? The question sounds so simple, but it's not. Your ideas should be put in writing if you are to get them properly sorted out. Most people keep a running list in their heads of what they want and work their way along by making selections from this mental list, adding and subtracting items from time to time. This natural system works well, and it certainly beats having no system (or no objectives) at all. However, you may have trouble keeping track of *all* the different ideas that make up your spending objectives. What's more, you'll have real trouble seeing how these objectives stack up in relation to each other. You may not get around to thinking how you can satisfy your wants in some way other than spending money. Without a means to analyze and compare various spending events and outcomes you'll have no way at all to measure the progress you're making in effective spending as time goes by.

Yes, it's time for another list.

This list will help you solve the problem of setting priorities and deciding which goals to pursue first. It will help you see how much you can have at any one time and show the best way to get what you want with the least amount of money. Here is how you can set up this list.

WORKSHEET FOR SIX-MONTH PLANNING

ITEM	ROOTS REVIEW	SUBSTITUTION?	TIMING

Start this list by writing in the Item column those things you think you want the most now. This is the time to refer back to the lists you wrote in Chapter Two.

Those lists were divided into four categories: Security, Caring for Others, Buyables, and Leisure. When you made them up you may have marked a few of the items you wanted the very most. Review your lists and select a total of up to ten items from the four lists. You don't have to set a quota for yourself or make a balanced selection among the four categories. Just pick the ones you want now or in the near future. You should restrict yourself, however, to what you may be able to accomplish in the next six months. If some things are big items, you may want to start saving money to pay for them. You may need to juggle your priorities back and forth for a while before you set a dollar amount to allot each month toward big objectives.

You'll notice this list doesn't have a space for the cost of the individual items. When you've made your decisions, you can set the amount of time you plan to take to accomplish your objective and then match this to the dollars available to you. Your Monthly Audit should give you enough information to understand what you may be able to spend. When you find out the exact cost of the best bargain you can make for your objective, add it in the Item column alongside that objective.

Don't agonize over the items, their order or their value. Planning is a flexible practice, not an ironclad regime to which you'll be irrevocably committed.

Once you've filled in the Item column of your worksheet, you're ready to start reviewing your decisions. To help you understand the review process, I've set up my own current list as an example to review along with you. Here are the items I selected:

* Security: Retirement investments.
* Caring for Others: Help catalogue local historic sites.
* Buyables: Improve wardrobe; vacation in Northwest; set up home library.
* Leisure: Dance classes; visit two friends.

My list may be very different from yours. Nonetheless, after you have made out your list I think you will discover that you have some of the same problems in setting priorities that I do and can use some of the same kinds of solutions.

Even with a list that is narrowed down to selected items and that includes only the next six months, there are bound to be conflicts. You and I can't do everything we want, but we are going to have to look at our motivations and at possible trade-offs, and thereby provide as much satisfaction for ourselves as we can.

First, we'll review spending "roots" to be doubly sure that what we think we want isn't just a response to some of our programming. You may want to look again at Chapter Three. You don't want to obey thoughtlessly the dicta of masculinity or femininity. You don't need to follow blindly the conventions of the generation in which you grew up or the attitudes about money that are held by your parents or other members of your family. Most of all, you should be in charge of your own life. The planning worksheet is an excellent way to avoid decisions-by-default. There are few things you really do need, and so you should be free to make choices about the rest.

Let's get on with our lists. If you look back at my list, you may think I am going overboard on the first item, Security. I want to improve my retirement income with some investments. If you are remembering what I said about generational differences, you may be thinking that I grew up in a security-hungry generation. Yes, I did. However, my programming leaned heavily toward the idea that I should get a civil service job, and then a good pension would provide for me. I've got a lot of time in with a good retirement system, and my husband has even more. But inflation has changed things, and the pensions won't be enough to buy extras we know we'll want.

Have my spending roots influenced any of my other selections? They really shouldn't have, because I've used a planning worksheet and thought through my spending objectives many times. Nonetheless, when I went through my list a second time, I found one item that made me say "Aha!" It was the dance classes.

I want these dance classes mainly for physical fitness and fun, but I caught myself thinking " . . . and when you go out, you ought to be able to keep up with all the latest dance styles." Every time you think the phrase *you ought,* go on the alert. Those two words are often a signal that you are making plans in response to what you've been programmed to do. This response may or may not be in keeping with the goals that are now most important to you. Ask yourself the next question. Why?

If you get an answer that's the equivalent of *just because* you'll know you are getting somewhere. I found I was getting a *just because* answer when I asked myself why I should be able to do all the latest dances. I think this is left over from my adolescent years when it was very important to be able to fit in with what everybody (all the other kids) did. Being able to fit in with the crowd isn't as important as some of the other objectives in my current situation. I'll keep on thinking about those dance classes because I expect I would enjoy them, but this is one item I'm willing to postpone in order to have a better chance to achieve my other immediate goals.

When you give your list the roots review, mull over each item long enough to listen to whatever thoughts drift into your head. Stay especially alert for influences that may be guiding you into spending decisions that won't serve the needs you now have.

Above all, don't plan your spending to conform to the ideas of others about what you should want. Don't make a purchase because the person selling something has been particularly pleasant or persistent or has given you the idea that you're obliged to buy from him or her. Don't be reassured that you can afford something because someone has been willing to approve your credit.

For all of the items that pass muster, put an OK in your Roots Review column.

Next, we should examine our lists to find the ways we can achieve goals without spending money needlessly or sooner than is necessary. Use the Substitution column for this.

Often (though not always) the substitute for money can be time. In going through my list I found two items for which a substitution could be made. The first had to do with improving my wardrobe. The honest translation for that item is that most of my summer clothes were a good fit about ten pounds ago. I need to decide whether to spend money or lose weight. The second substitution has to do with wanting to set up my home library.

I started out thinking about the price of shelving. Then I wandered off into a fine expensive daydream about getting one of those old-fashioned library ladders. With the right antique hardware I could fit up a rack to slide back and forth across floor-to-ceiling shelves in one room of our big old house. The bookshelves in this daydream, of course, are filled with my books which I have put in perfect order. My daydream lingers here, on the wondrous order of my books. Well! Here's a piece of what I want that I can achieve without spending money. I can put some organization into my helter-skelter book collection. I'm going to have to give myself the carrot-and-stick approach with this one: I can't spend the money until I've sorted the doggone books.

Give yourself time to do some mental meandering about what you really want to accomplish with those items on your list. Daydream or think ahead a bit. Be honest with yourself, especially if you think you may be using the spending of money as a goad to get yourself to do something else. Find the key elements in what you really want, and then see what substitutions of time or effort you can make to achieve those key elements. Mark the possible substitutions on your list. If no substitutions come to mind, perhaps spending money *is* essential to your goal.

Now you are ready to decide about timing. Look at the money available and decide on the time sequence or intervals. On my list, I've already decided to start the retirement investment right away. As to the historic building survey, I think I'd better wait about two months and see how my supply of time is working out. This project will take very little money, but I have to be sure it doesn't take time I would prefer to spend somewhere else. This will relate to the progress of my book sorting. I'll mark the historic building project for a decision in two months.

Two months is also the time interval I'll allot myself for deciding about getting some new summer clothes. Four months from now should be just about right for deciding about that vacation, or at least how long we'll stay and in what style we'll travel. By then I'll have made a decision about summer clothes and have more information about how much money I'll spend for my library project and how soon I'll spend it.

As to visiting my friends, I'll take action right now. These two people have been very important in my life, but except for Christmas cards and a few letters I've been out of touch for too long. Yet I know I have other priorities for my time and money and won't be traveling to see them this year. I'll get in touch with each of them by telephone and be content to pay that oversized phone bill when it comes in. I can do it right away because most of my other decisions don't call for spending money until a little later.

When you've finished filling in your Worksheet for Six-Month Planning, you should feel pretty good about yourself and very much in charge of your affairs. I always do when I've worked out a list, even though I know from experience I'll make changes before the six months are out. Here's what my list looked like when I got through with it.

ITEM	ROOTS REVIEW	SUBSTITUTION?	TIMING
Retirement investments ($100 per month)	OK	—	Now
Help catalogue local historic sites	OK	—	Two months
Improve wardrobe	OK	Lose weight?	Two months
Vacation in Northwest	OK	—	Four months
Set up home library	OK	Sort books	Four months
Dance classes	Aha!	Exercise	—
Visit two friends	OK	Phone	Now

I hope that now you understand some of the advantages of setting your priorities in writing and then scheduling times to make decisions about them. Your list can save you a lot of worry, prevent feelings of guilt or inadequacy about something you haven't yet done, and stop the squirrel-cage thinking that can come from trying to plan and do everything in one chunk.

Getting your plans down on paper means that you won't be doing that juggling act of trying to carry everything in your head. You will have your ideas in writing so that you can look at each of them in turn. You can examine your objectives to locate the key elements — the aspects of them that are most important to you. This will help you spend in ways that are most in keeping with who you truly are and what you really want.

Having a written plan filed away with your monthly audit is a great help in keeping your objectives firmly in mind. You can measure impulsive spending temptations against the plan you've made. You'll know what it is that those salespeople are trying to "steal" from you. On the other hand, your circumstances may change. If you wait a while you may decide to pursue an objective that has recently become more important.

You've made your start on successful spending by taking two important steps. The first was doing your Monthly Audit. This means you now have your guideposts, those totals that let you know how you're doing and how much progress you're making in dollars and cents as the months roll along. The second step is making your Categorized List of Objectives, the things you want most to do or have. I imagine you may already have identified some aimless, unrewarding, or deferrable spending you can give up in order to achieve these goals more quickly.

Remember, don't feel badly if you don't accomplish each and every goal. I know from experience I won't. However, we will both be spending more successfully than we would without a plan. We'll each improve our planning skills as we continue to practice them.

Later we're going to talk about setting short- and long-term goals and integrating these goals with those of other people in your life. We'll also talk about the proper uses of frugality and the supposedly frugal measures that don't accomplish anything at all. We'll review the tactics for successful shopping, and I'll show you some ways for turning your big dreams into future reality. But first we're going to learn about the many ways in which spending can go wrong, the mistakes that are so easy to make. You won't be likely to make them if you know what they are. That's what the second section of this book is about.

PART II

Money Traps

and How to Avoid Them

5.

The Common Practice
of Brinksmanship

THE BEST WAY that I know to explain brinksmanship is to tell you about someone who was caught up in one form of this particular money trap.

On first impression you wouldn't think Esther Brown had a care in the world. She's petite, with sleek curly brown hair framing her even, delicate features. Her figure is generous but trim, and she has impeccable taste in classic sports clothes. Esther was divorced only last year from her Army officer husband, and she helps support her twin eight-year-old daughters with a job in a fashionable tourist center selling turquoise and silver jewelry.

Esther has tried to be very careful about the financial decisions she's made, but nonetheless she's become uneasy about how she will be able to make ends meet on her salary and the child-support payments from her former husband. She shopped diligently to find a modest apartment in a nice neighborhood. She agonized over the decision to send her daughters to a private school but felt it was necessary. Her charge account balance at the local department store is creeping upward, mostly because of clothes and shoes she feels the girls must have.

In her continuing effort to stay solvent, she's dropped the insurance on her car. The car became hers with the divorce, along with payments on it that must be continued for another year. She's hoping to make it through that year, and then she thinks she will have a better chance at staying even financially.

Esther knows she's in a spot in which she can't afford one misstep, but this night she's especially worried. Her former husband's younger brother is in town. Anxious to demonstrate to his family that she bears them no grudge over the divorce, she's loaned the young man her car. It's getting late, and she's wondering whether she should have asked him if he had insurance. The girls went to bed hours ago, and Esther will feel much relieved when she hears the sound of the car engine in the parking lot. Instead, the phone rings . . .

For Esther the news is all bad. Her former brother-in-law was unaware of a badly worn front tire. At the same time he was eager to test the limits of the car. The tire blew as he rounded a curve on the interstate north of town, sending the car out of control and into a utility pole.

Don't worry, the young man tells her; he's not hurt except for minor injuries. No other cars were involved. Insurance? No, he doesn't have any because he doesn't own a car.

Esther is now in serious trouble.

What happened to Esther might happen to any of us, or at least to a large number of us. Esther was practicing brinksmanship, and she fell into this commonest of all money traps.

What exactly is brinksmanship?

It's living on the narrow margin of financial disaster. William Buckner of the Home Economics Department of California State University, Long Beach, first explained the concept to me. Buckner is an attorney and also the founder and director of the Long Beach Financial Crisis Clinic.

"Few people are aware of how insecure their personal income can be or of how close they may be to the brink of financial disaster," Buckner tells me.

"Many people don't even have so much as the amount of one paycheck standing between themselves and deep trouble. All it takes is to miss that one paycheck, to be surprised by one major setback or illness, and over the edge they go."

Buckner points out that brinksmanship is more often practiced among middle or higher income people.

"People with lower incomes usually concentrate on the basics of surviving. They know they don't have means to get more," Buckner says.

He points out that people with higher incomes often don't fully understand what they can and cannot afford. The choices available to these people, he says, are more confusing to them.

"They may feel that a certain lifestyle is essential to their self-esteem," he explains. "When we work with people at our crisis counseling clinic, the most important objective is to guide them toward rebuilding their self-esteem — and to help them know what they don't need to buy to maintain it."

Why does this business of trying to maintain or achieve a certain lifestyle trip up so many people? "Before the escalation of inflation, it simply wasn't acceptable to most people to try to have the good life on the time payment plan," Buckner says. "Now the guidelines are not so clear. It's hard to tell whether you are just buying something before the price goes up again or whether you are living beyond your means. Nowadays there are fewer ways to know what people can reasonably expect at specific incomes and stages in life. More money leads to the possibility for higher expectations, and that's where the problems come."

When he works with the people who come to his financial clinic, Buckner may start by describing the geography of brinksmanship.

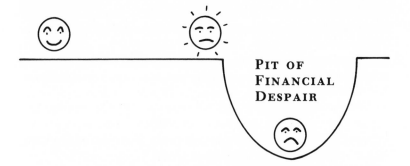

"Far back from the edge of the Pit of Financial Despair is the person who is relatively secure, who keeps plenty of distance from the edge," Buckner says. "Yet many people are poised right on the brink, and quite often they are unaware of their dangerous situation."

Is Esther Brown's situation typical of the distress that can come from practicing brinksmanship? "Absolutely," says Buckner. "Loaning a car is typical of the event that may push people over the edge. Also typical is owning a dog that bites someone, someone who decides to sue."

Lack of insurance is often involved, according to Buckner, as are problems with child support — whether the person in financial trouble is the one who must make payments or the one who is struggling to make ends meet on those payments.

"More often," Buckner says, "it is not the one dramatic event that pushes people into the Pit of Financial Despair but rather an accumulation of events. Plans must be made to allow for owning a pet, operating a car, paying for home repairs, or taking care of additional family members. Housing costs, food, and utilities are constantly going up. When there is no money at the moment to pay for them, these routine expenses become debts."

How do financial counselors work with people like Esther Brown who have come face-to-face with financial calamity? Buckner starts with an analysis of the person's current financial situation.

"After this we go on to identify specifically the kinds of problems that person has — income problems, living expense problems, and debt problems," he says. "Like many people in financial trouble, Esther has all three problems.

When Buckner analyzes Esther's financial situation, he says it is typical of women who find themselves suddenly faced with the necessity of earning a living. "Her job situation is quite characteristic. Her work is socially very acceptable, but her pay is low," he explains. "Her earnings plus the money from child support payments just don't provide enough money to maintain her in a lifestyle she considers minimal."

He adds that the incident with the car will increase her immediate problems. "The loss of the car will interfere with her ability to work. Once the repair work on the car is done, she will not have the means to pay for it. What's more, she'll likely face a claim from the utility company for the cost of replacing the pole and possibly other claims for damage caused. She is the registered owner of the vehicle that was responsible."

Buckner points out that Esther's situation, even without the added difficulty of the accident, is common among people who are trying to hold on to some elements of a former lifestyle. "To sum it up," he says, "she can't afford to live as she has been trying to live."

He says that a common difficulty for people like Esther is their income problem, and that this generates both living-expense and debt problems.

"Living expenses month-to-month are not debts, nor are they ever paid off. You continue to have to pay for housing, the groceries, and transportation. However, past-due living expenses become debts. This is what's happened in Esther's situation. Her living expense problems have spilled over and become debt problems."

He has found that it's common among people with financial difficulties to feel that they have only debt problems. "I remember one man who was spending $400 a month eating in restaurants, and couldn't pay his bills. He thought he had a debt problem, but we had to point out to him that he had a living expense problem. That's why we try to help identify particular problems, whether they are income problems, living expense problems, or debts."

Regarding Esther's situation, Buckner points out that an assessment will show where she must look for solutions. What can Esther do? Obviously, she'll have to increase her income, cut down on her living expenses, or both. In her case, a credit counselor might explore with her the possibility that she try for an increase in the child-support payments, or ask her former husband or perhaps the twins' grandparents for some specific help with school expenses or other needs. Now that she understands how inadequate her income is, she may find the courage to make an effective bid for more money or to begin looking for a job that will pay her a better salary.

As to coping with her expenses, she may have to relocate

somewhere so that she can walk to work, or consider taking in someone to share the rental costs. These options were open to her all along, but she may not have perceived them or may not have felt they were acceptable because she didn't fully understand her financial situation.

Financial counselors, Buckner says, can offer another kind of specific help to Esther and to other people in similar circumstances. They can help her cope with the kind of pressures she is now likely to face: harassment for payment of delinquent debts, cuts in services for unpaid bills, possible repossession of belongings, and also the possibility of lawsuits that may lead to garnishments and the taking of property. He explains that he would have to discuss with someone like Esther how these events will affect her.

"Some people aren't bothered by dunning phone calls, bill collectors pounding on the door, or other such things," he says, "but others are absolutely terrified. Esther may eventually need the services of a lawyer, but she should first seek the help of a consumer credit counselor. Lawyers are not necessarily experienced in this kind of thing and tend to think strictly in terms of legal remedies."

Many in the legal profession are aware of this. Here is how the situation is described in a statement published under the auspices of the California State Bar Association.

"Regardless of how a debtor contacted the law office, it may soon become apparent that the debtor's problems are not the kind for legal resolution. An attorney is not a consumer affairs specialist or a professional debt counselor. Frequently the person consulting an attorney about a desperate debt problem needs immediate debt counseling, e.g., setting up realistic debt repayment schedules, budgeting family income, scaling down conspicuous spending, etc. These cases should be referred to the appropriate consumer affairs or voluntary agencies listed in the telephone directory."

Buckner suggests that people in financial trouble similar to Esther Brown's check the yellow pages of their local directory for the kind of help they need. (A listing of consumer credit counselors is also available from the National Foundation for

Consumer Credit, Inc., Federal Building West, 1819 H Street NW, Washington, D.C. 20006.)

The work at Buckner's financial counseling clinic has verified over and over again one very important point about brinksmanship and bankruptcy. One of the major causes of financial woe is spending that is dictated by what people feel they ought to do.

According to Buckner there are many kinds of expenditures that are unwise in individual financial situations, but the people who make them feel guilty if they don't spend in such ways.

"This was one element in Esther Brown's problem," he says. "She was doing what she felt she ought to do, the 'right' thing, even if she did not have the resources to do it. This contradicts a popular notion about people with money problems. Too often people think of a bankrupt person as someone who has no self-control and has gotten into trouble trying to satisfy every desire and every whim — that a childish impulsiveness and lack of responsibility underlies the problem. This isn't true in a great number of cases. Esther Brown is just one example."

He says that it has been traditional to talk about the distinction between needs and wants. "In the work at our clinic, however, we've identified a third element: oughts."

Buckner defines needs as items like food or rent and wants as things like travel and other luxuries. "The oughts can include a new car when the existing one is quite adequate because there's the feeling that this is appropriate. We are all programmed to dress in a certain fashion, live in a certain type of neighborhood, and so forth. We ask the people we counsel to identify their own motivations and think through whether the expenditures they're making are for needs, wants, or oughts."

Buckner illustrates this point well from his own experience. "When we are influenced by the 'ought' factor we are trying to avoid being given 'that look,'" he says.

He recalls an early encounter with "that look." "I was still in high school," he says. "There was a formal dance. It happened that I wore the same size jacket as my father, and he offered to loan me a formal jacket that he had bought a few years earlier. At the dance, everything went fine for me and for my date until another girl asked why I was wearing a tux that was out of style. Suddenly I was getting 'that look' from my date. I wanted to hide."

Buckner says he now understands that the comment about his jacket was not just about the garment but about him as the person wearing it. "Such comments give us an image of ourselves that we find difficult to tolerate, especially when we are not prepared for it," he says.

Buckner still gets 'that look' from time to time. "Not long ago I went to a meeting with a number of attorneys," he explains. "Afterward, another lawyer and I walked out to the parking lot together. As he started to get into his expensive car, he asked me where mine was. I indicated the low-status economy car parked right next to his Cadillac. He gave me a look of astonishment. People — the look they get on their faces sometimes — you're constantly bombarded."

Buckner says it's no longer difficult for him to cope with such looks. "But it's taken me a while," he says. "You have to feel secure about yourself and your reasons for doing what you do. Many of us don't like the mental image of ourselves in, for instance, a cheapie car. We will spend money on something like a car or expensive clothes, yet this kind of expenditure can contribute only to an external evaluation of ourselves. We should instead make our own internal evaluation of our worth. That's the evaluation that really counts."

Once you have established your own evaluation of yourself you will find it much easier to sort out the reasons why you are spending some of your money, and you are likely to feel less pressured to spend in ways that contribute to an external evaluation of your worth. You will be able to distinguish the situations in which outer appearances are essential from the situations in which the spending serves only to enhance your self-image.

Are you sometimes caught in the trap of trying to do what you ought — of trying to avoid "that look" — even when you can scarcely afford it? I suspect you're well able to recognize a "you ought" situation when you find yourself in one. Nonetheless, here is a litany of the typical "you oughts" that can push people into financial trouble:

* You ought to loan something to a relative who needs it.
* You ought to provide a fine wedding, funeral, or graduation gift.
* You ought never to let a friend down.
* You ought to forget about money when someone is gravely ill.
* You ought to have a home that reflects your good taste and your financial status.
* You ought always to keep up appearances.
* You ought to give your kids the things you never had.
* You ought always to make the same contribution as everyone else.
* You ought to spend money to prove how much you care.

No one wants to get stuck with a host of obligations — with ruined dreams and no choices. No one wants to spend a couple of years just getting back to square one. An understanding of the influence of the "you oughts" is but one of many insights that can help you avoid brinksmanship and the difficulties it can engender. The more you know about brinksmanship, the better you will be able to avoid it. What are some other ways in which you can tell if you're vulnerable to a brinksmanship style?

There are guidelines and danger signals you should keep in mind. People who are beyond their individual safety margin often exhibit certain styles of thinking. Here are some of the thought habits typical of people dangerously near the brink of financial disaster:

* A pursuit of ignorance. Remember my friend who didn't want to look at his bank statement? This type of thinking can also emerge as an attitude of "If I want it I'll buy it; don't tell me the price." It can mean an unwillingness to shop carefully, to explore alternatives, to examine motivations for buying, or to postpone purchases. It means a general refusal to take stock of the financial situation. It can also mean thinking of persistent financial troubles as merely a series of isolated instances. Among those for whom this is the mode you'll hear comments such as: "It's just this

once;" "It's only temporary;" "This is a special circumstance."

* A tendency to see someone else or some outside influence as the cause of the immediate problem. Those who fall into this trap may see themselves as otherwise modest spenders who must yield to the extravagant wishes of others in the family. (But they participate in the enjoyment of those purchases.) Even when they haven't paid for necessary upkeep on the car they are likely to see an untimely breakdown as bad luck. If an accident or illness interrupts the flow of paychecks and they have no reserve, this, too, is misfortune.

* A habit of living as if there were no tomorrow. Among some people with severe money problems, I've seen this operate as a way of life. If the landlord has been told the rent will be paid next Monday, there's no problem until Monday rolls around and the landlord must be persuaded to believe something else. If there isn't money to put new heels on a pair of shoes, they'll be worn until they're ruined, and the cost of a new pair will be dealt with later. Until there's no gas for the car, no food in the cupboard, and no cash available, some people let tomorrow take care of itself because they have enough other things to worry about today. Some people at higher income levels also have the no-tomorrow style. If so, they tend to think they can afford what they want as long as the limit on credit cards hasn't been reached. They may try to resolve immediate money problems by postponing or ignoring insurance on the car or trips to the dentist. They may avoid thinking about that income tax bite that's going to come because they opted for a smaller income tax deduction from their paycheck.

If these styles — the pursuit of ignorance, blaming outside influences, or the no-tomorrow approach — have characterized your attitudes about money, you may be nearer than you realize to the brink of that Pit of Financial Despair.

How much distance should you keep from the brink? The answer will vary with your circumstances. You may not need much in the way of financial backstopping if, for instance, you are unmarried and a recent college graduate with an exciting new job. However, you'll need much, much more reserve if you have more obligations, perhaps a spouse or children who rely on you for support, or an elderly parent. You'll also need more if you have health problems or if you are coming close to retirement and will soon have to settle for monthly checks that are small in size and relatively fixed in amount. You may be somewhere in the midrange if there are two wage earners in the family or if there is a job that is especially secure, perhaps with a generous supply of sick leave or vacation accumulated.

Is your debt load very high? There is a rule-of-thumb for installment debts (including your automobile). You are safe if such debts are ten percent or less of your take-home pay, in wobbly circumstances if they total about fifteen percent of that paycheck, and in serious trouble if they are up to twenty percent. Maybe these guidelines are realistic for you and maybe not. Consider them carefully in the light of your own circumstances.

How much do you have in savings or in assets that can quickly be converted to cash? The conservative standard is that you should be able to come up with an amount equal to six months' pay. I suspect this guideline applies to the so-called average family with a breadwinner, housewife, and two children. That brand-new college graduate with a marketable degree probably doesn't need as much in savings, but for some families, those with many dependents or an irregular income, it might scarcely be a prudent minimum. Again, review your circumstances. Think what you might do if you had to miss one paycheck . . . or two . . . or three.

Now you have the guidelines. However, you must decide for yourself how to avoid that money trap known as brinksmanship. If you have been dangerously close to the brink and have only now become aware of your circumstances, perhaps you will want to put the setting up of a reserve fund as a top-priority item in your spending plans.

6.

Spender,
Know Thyself

SOMETIMES WE SET money traps for ourselves because of quirks in our approach to spending. Sometimes we don't know how to cope with advertising pressures. Sometimes we don't communicate effectively with others. All of these can add up to dollars gone astray. Yet an understanding of these things, plus some tactics for countering them, can help put us on the road toward using our money for what we really want to have and do.

A look at behavior in the animal kingdom may help us to understand just one of the many spending quirks humans are subject to.

Some time ago a group of scientists observed gorillas in their natural surroundings. When it rained, the researchers found that the gorillas didn't like to get wet. In the setting in which the animals were watched, the shelter of the forest was available to them. But if a group of gorillas were in a clearing when a rain shower began, they did not seek the cover of the trees. Instead, they huddled together in misery, their shoulders drawn up and their heads pulled down, waiting abjectly for the rain to stop.

Sometimes when unpleasantness comes along, people will behave like gorillas in the rain. They won't take action to seek out any of the alternatives available to them, but instead passively endure the problem until it's ended.

Behaving like a gorilla in the rain can cost money if passivity leads us to stick with a spending decision that has no real benefit. It could be a subscription to an expensive series of books, the payments for which later cut into our money supply. Maybe it's signing up for some instruction — a course to get a contractor's license, for example — and then discovering it's just not going to be the right thing to do. Most likely, we go on with the no-longer-wanted obligation, waiting it out until the darn bill is paid and the sun shines for us again. When you find yourself caught in an unwanted arrangement, you don't have to sit it out. You can do something about it. This may bruise your ego. However, you may bruise your ego even more if you don't do anything.

If you catch yourself making a Gorilla-in-the-rain mistake, have a laugh if you want. You can even shout, "I made a mistake!" If you're having a good time, shout some more: "So what! I don't have to keep on making that mistake!" You may feel silly, but it's a lot better than sitting in the rain. Most important, you'll salvage some dollars to put to use for something you really want.

Maybe you're not subject to gorilla-in-the-rain mistakes, but you may be setting some other money traps for yourself. Are you one of those people who isn't content unless something is done perfectly? Perfection, if you achieve it, may be causing you to sacrifice some other goals that are more important to you. Perfectionism in one area is always accomplished at some loss elsewhere.

For instance, when you shop for clothes, do you let the high-style atmosphere of the department store coerce you into thinking you need a perfect ensemble instead of just that one pair of slacks you set out to get? Did you buy all new fireplace equipment when all that was needed was a replacement for a broken set of tongs? If you took your car to the dealer because the door handle needed replacing, did you find yourself feeling uneasy about your merely adequate means of transportation? You may be giving up some other important goals if you give in to a perfectionist inclination.

If you're tempted to make a purchase to satisfy these perfectionist impulses, make your best guess about how much extra you will have to spend when something less-than-perfect would serve your basic purposes. Then decide what else you'd rather do with the money.

The self-esteem dilemma is closely related to the perfectionist problem. In most of us at least part of our self-esteem is geared to the material quality of our surroundings. There is no denying the value of good first impressions, but we can easily become persuaded to overrate the value of a perfectly kept environment or an uncompromisingly fashionable wardrobe. Sometimes we are unable to think well of ourselves if the upholstery on the living room couch is worn, if our clothes are ill-fitting or out-of-date, or if our car carries an accumulation of rusted dents and a tail-light held on with masking tape. We refuse to believe that others will think we are trying to conserve money. Instead we respond as if we're sure they're thinking we're lazy or just don't know any better. We're afraid of getting "that look" that William Buckner talked about.

Do you think you need to have everything in your environment arranged to meet the highest standards of others? You will, of course, want to have your personal surroundings reasonably well maintained. It may, in fact, be that getting your home or yourself in order will serve as an excellent morale booster. Nonetheless *you* should be in charge. *You* should be making the decisions rather than acting in response to the notion that you must always have topnotch clothes, household furnishings, and car.

Let me share with you a person I invented. Her name is Mrs. Asperdiddlehammer. I think everyone has his own version of Mrs. Asperdiddlehammer. For me, she is the fictitious individual who clucks disapprovingly on a morning when I go directly to work on an interesting project instead of first making the bed and cleaning up the breakfast things. She looks over my shoulder when I'm in the stationery store to buy Christmas cards and think of passing up the luxurious ones in favor of a more economical design. She scowls at me when I get an invitation to a wedding and consider wearing that same outfit one more time.

It's taken me a long while to learn to thumb my nose at Mrs.

Asperdiddlehammer. The reason I can is because I know I've got other things, more important to me, to do with my time and money. I don't have to do what she, or some mysterious "they," think is appropriate.

Another money trap involves what I call Up-Down spending. None of us manages to keep our moods and our spending on an absolutely even keel, and we probably shouldn't want to. However, too many ups and downs can be costly. What happens with Up-Down spending at its worst are wild swings between letting it all hang out and austerity campaigns.

Let's look first at what can happen in one of those spending surges. This is a time when you're likely to keep yourself ignorant of the real latitude you have for spending or choose to ignore limits you know perfectly well. You may embark on an unneeded redecorating job, throw an expensive party, or start shopping for something that will cost a lot of money.

I'm not recommending that you put a damper on these marvelous up times, just that you learn to express them in a different way at least some of the time. Arrange a picnic instead of a night on the town, for instance, or use your abundant energies for a closet-cleaning spree. Haul out all of your unused items and have a garage sale. This is a perfect time to dig in and weed the yard.

When it's time to make up for a spending surge, you'll likely lose money, too. Maybe it won't hurt to leave those clothes at the cleaners until you can afford to pick them up. It may even be beneficial to discover how many meals can be improvised out of whatever is in the cupboard. But what about extra interest you may have to pay if there's barely enough for the minimum on your charge accounts? You may even have to cut down on needed maintenance on your home or car, or for that matter, your health. The most costly consequence? The expenses you've incurred may mean that someone in your family will unjustly have to do without — a circumstance that's certain to bring a negative reaction that will eventually take it's toll on family relationships.

Here's another spending pattern. If you sometimes feel that you're headed off in all directions at once, zigzagging could be your problem. In everyone's life there should be times for exploration, for trying out this goal and that activity. Sometimes, however, as in the case of Susan Wavering, zig follows zag with bewildering rapidity, and the exploration does not seem to yield any refinement of direction or depth of purpose.

How can you tell if you're in a zigzag pattern that goes far beyond healthy exploration? Here are some criteria:

* Your spending is often impulsive and spur-of-the-moment.
* The notion to try this or that is more often an attempt to relieve boredom than to test out some goal.
* You never continue very long in any direction.
* The idea of what to try is generated by someone else. You may be following someone's suggestion, or you may be imitating someone.
* You usually have the exaggerated expectation that this is the activity or possession that's really going to make you happy, but your anticipated joy fades even before the activity is completed or shortly after you've acquired the possession.

Here's another idea to help you understand your spending patterns. Consider that sometimes you act in accordance with a careful and ordered style of thinking and other times you follow your intuitive, creative perceptions. Some people make spending mistakes when they allow logical thinking to override their instincts.

Has this happened to you?

For instance, it could have been a vacation. You'd been hard at work or involved in extensive projects. You wanted to continue, but the calendar said it was time for a vacation and your travel agent suggested a place that was ideal to visit at that time of year and a bargain to boot. All logic said it was time to pack up and go, but you were dragging your feet. Maybe you let your instinctive feelings that you weren't ready for a vacation be overruled. If so, you probably walked through a vacation that could have been much more enjoyable if you'd waited until you were ready to take it.

Your intuition could be holding up some action you're now

considering, perhaps an investment. All conventional reason says buy those stocks or invest in that duplex. Yet, you don't know why, you've been letting the money sit in a savings account. It could be that you are just very busy and preoccupied with other things. It may just be, however, that the intuitive part of your mind is trying to tell you something. Should you ignore those subliminal signals and tie up your money? Perhaps. But perhaps there is some reason why you *should* keep your money readily available. Some event may be about to occur in your life that is unexpected by all logical standards but not to the inner workings of your mind.

When it comes to spending decisions, consider that if something you are about to do *feels* like a mistake, it may *be* a mistake. If you have mixed feelings about spending decisions, give them further thought. Mull things over and see if you can pin down what's making you feel hesitant. If you've made any "I felt uneasy about this" spending decisions recently, make a note to keep track of the situation. As time goes by, you should gain some useful insights into how your intuition works.

ADVERTISING PRESSURES

We can save a lot of money by understanding the concepts behind advertising and how they are designed to persuade us to buy. This understanding can help us resist advertising for things we don't need or really want.

Just how big a business is advertising? It accounts for two-and-a-half percent of our entire Gross National Product, and that's exclusive of in-person selling. Advertising does serve to provide information to consumers. However, we often pay more for advertising than the value of the information we get.

Some advertising is downright practical. Most of us, for instance, appreciate the supermarket ads we see in the weekly newspaper food pages. We can sit down if we choose, compare prices, and plot our food shopping tactics. But there's much more advertising we recognize as subterfuge. We know it uses fantasy and other means to persuade us to buy. This is the advertising we need to understand.

Advertisers work hard to get us to part with our dollars.

Obviously, if advertising weren't effective it wouldn't continue to be used. Advertising can appeal to our dreams, to our fears, and to our need to be accepted by others. Here are some of the standard advertising approaches.

Image and Association. This has got to be the all-time champion top-of-the-heap advertising ploy. Think about some of those television commercials you've seen. There was one with a long-haired, long-legged beauty running in slow motion. Her hair, shampooed with the right product, flowed in the breeze. Her lover, equally good-looking, was running to greet her. There was the one for sunglasses, I think, that showed a handsome young author seated at an outdoor cafe in a tropical resort, presumably tapping out the words of his next trendy novel on the portable typewriter in his lap even while he carried on fascinating conversations with the others in his group. Always, there are all those liquor ads showing beautiful people in provocative situations and suggesting that alcohol (the sponsors' brand) will make wonderful things happen.

We know that a slug of booze won't clothe us in glamorous evening dress or turn us into sexual bombshells. We know that using a certain product won't cause us to become as stylish as that handsome author. We don't really believe that using a particular shampoo will transform us into that lissome girl with her hair flowing in the breeze. Nonetheless, this kind of advertising appeals to that streak of wishful, wistful thinking in all of us — that willingness to hope that some kind of magic will work for us if we buy as we are sold.

This kind of advertising seeks to work on an ideal self-image and then attach the product to it. This is why the ad writers often associate the product with a creative, exotic, or otherwise out-of-the-ordinary setting. Then, too, these ads play on everyone's desire to be upwardly mobile. That's why they show the deodorant user as a young architect presenting construction plans at an executive meeting. In this kind of ad we don't see any successfully deodorized motel maids, fry cooks, or garbage collectors. And if the people in these ads don't have leadership status, they have some other quality with which people may want to identify. One example is the magnificently outdoorsy men in the beer or cigarette ads. These, of course, are aimed specifically at an image of male virility. Use our product, they tell men, and you will be successful in the way these men are successful — muscular, admired by women, and most definitely one of the boys.

In dealing with image and association advertising, I've developed my own strategy for immunity: I substitute something else for the product in question. Suppose that product is a certain line of cosmetics. The ads suggest that my use of the lipsticks, nail polish, or mascara will help transform me into a beauty who strolls windswept moors, frequents European spas or expensive shopping districts, and invariably is involved in situations with handsome men.

If I catch myself beginning to believe that I might do what that model is portrayed doing, I put my substitution imagery to work. Rather than cosmetics I imagine the product is a long, fat, dark, ugly cigar. As soon as I mentally put El Cheapo Cigar in the mouth of that beautiful girl, the magic disappears in a puff of smoke.

Try it. This trick works wonders on all those image and association ads, whether they're for expensive sports cars, a new line of lacy underwear, or an exotic after-dinner drink.

Perhaps the El Cheapo Cigar image won't work as well for men who think they may be influenced by the macho beer ads or similar promotions. Men will have to develop their own version of the cigar. Maybe those ham-fisted men in the macho ads can be imagined putting pink ribbons in their hair instead of clutching beer cans.

Scare Tactics. Do you remember the ads for chain link fencing? They feature dramatizations suggesting that a family's dog may be run down in the street or a child may stray away from home unless this fencing is bought. These ads work on a very straightforward fear for the safety of family and possessions.

More often, the emotion evoked is fear of social disapproval. This kind of advertising plays on feelings much like William Buckner experienced when his out-of-date tux brought "that look" from his girlfriend. Yes, these ads include the ring-around-the-collar or dandruff-on-your-shoulder or person-in-the-elevator-who-didn't-use-deodorant scenarios. We can smile at such ads if we want, but we often set aside our sales resistance and buy what they're selling anyhow.

Once you start to think about the matter, you can learn to resist ads that so seriously tell you your personal life will be a fiasco if you don't use the product. Here's my system for resisting scare tactics.

Do you remember the ads that suggest an expensive disinfectant must be spread into every nook and cranny in the kitchen and bathroom, or dangerous germs will multiply? A nosey neighbor comes over, sniffing around and saying the house smells bad. These ads seem to be saying that she could show up at my house and then cross my name off her social lists if I don't use the right product. In real life, anyone who showed up and behaved like that would get *her* name crossed off *my* list. What's more, I can use my own nose to tell me whether my home needs an airing. I've long since learned, too, to substitute elbow grease and common sense for most of those specialized (and expensive) cleaning products.

Bandwagon Ads. These ads try to persuade us to do something or buy something just because a great many other people are doing it. They feature slogans such as "Over a Quarter Million Sold," "Twenty Thousand Frenchmen Can't Be Wrong," or just simply "Everybody's Doing It." You won't need to conjure up images to counteract this kind of advertising once you understand what it is. There are thousands of people who are addicted to drugs, convicted of murder, or waiting their turn in the bankruptcy courts, and you don't need to imitate their behavior. You can base spending decisions on the logic of the specific situation, not on what's popular.

"Feel Good" Ads. These promise you'll have warm feelings about yourself if you feed your cat a certain kind of expensive cat food or if you make a certain kind of baked goods for your children. Mainly you are supposed to feel good because you've chosen this way to express your love. For Heaven's sake, you're intelligent enough to figure out your own ways of expressing love and gaining self-esteem, especially after you understand what's going on with these ads.

Silly Products. The pet rock craze has recently resurfaced in a much more expensive form: the registered rock, with its own identification number, packaged in an expensive gift box, and bearing a twenty-dollar price tag. Silly products are often merchandised as gifts, even though personally made silly gifts give much more fun and express a much closer feeling. Sellers seem to believe that we will do almost anything except use our heads when we're trying to get a name crossed off of our gift lists. John Steinbeck once summed it up very well: "Some things are made to be used," he wrote, "and some are just made to be sold."

But there are many ways you're sold that are not so obvious. One example of this kind of manipulation occurs in the area of recreation. Let's consider how you are sold when you go to a theme park.

Jay Mechling, Professor of American Studies at the Davis campus of the University of California, has studied the Great America format. He reports that the controlled flow of pedestrian traffic as people explore a park "forces you into a sequence most likely to induce spending."

Some of the attractions are large, expensive to build, and dangerous in feeling, he says. "As visitors follow the sequence of the park, there's 'dangerous' and then 'safe.'" Mechling points out that food and other merchandise is invariably available in these safe areas. "You do the scary work and then you can reward yourself," he says.

"There's one more clincher in the operation," he adds. "Parks are for kids, and we all know it's okay to spend for kids."

I suspect that similar emotional manipulation occurs when you visit many resorts, restaurants, and other recreation spots. The operators of these businesses may be unaware of how the tactics work; they just know a successful way to run their particular enterprise. Other salespeople also know exactly when and how to use emotional manipulation. I remember the insurance salesman who, in the midst of a pitch for a life insurance policy, commented to my husband that "you don't want to be dependent on FRC — that's Friends, Relatives, and Charity — when you're old, do you?" I remember a door-to-door seller of household cleaning products looking me squarely in the eye and saying, "We all want to be the best housekeepers we possibly can, don't we?"

You should have become fairly immune to such ploys by now, because you're learning more all the time about how advertising and sales tactics work and the ways we've been programmed to behave. Nonetheless, you may want to imagine that you are equipped with a set of antennae to detect emotional manipulation. You may be surprised at the number of phrases and situations that set your antennae quivering. Remember, if it *feels* like manipulation, it probably *is* manipulation.

INTERACTING WITH OTHERS

Better self-understanding, better understanding of the situation in which you find yourself, and better communication with others in your life can help you save money. This can work in ways both small and large, and often we discover that seemingly small matters aren't that small after all.

Here's one "small" matter that can cost over five hundred dollars a year. It's the result of one of the many possible patterns that can evolve when people are reluctant to face an issue squarely or to speak up about everyday problems. It's the fast-food expedient.

Think of a typical weekday evening for a family with two school-age children. Supper has to be prepared and a host of other chores done. The easiest solution for the woman in such a family is to ask her husband to load the kids in the car and fetch supper from the nearest fast-food establishment. While they're out of the house, the laundry can be started, the living room tidied, clean sheets put on the bed, and the houseplants watered. Because there's little or no cleanup after supper, the woman will have time for more chores or perhaps for the children.

It's much easier for a woman in this situation to ask her husband to take the children to get food than it is for her to confront her family and ask for some help. In fact, she may not have considered that getting help with "her" chores was something she might do.

How common is this type of situation?

A group of nutrition education workers from lower income and middle income families were recently asked what they would do if they found a twenty-dollar bill and felt they could keep it. They were almost unanimous about how they would spend the money:

"Eat more meals out that week."

This answer came from a group of women who, by the nature of their jobs, were thoroughly acquainted with the difference in cost and nutrition between home-cooked and fast-food meals. What's more, their replies were consistent when the question was asked in a different form. What would the nutrition workers do if they discovered their money supply was short by twenty dollars?

"Our family would eat out less, and I would cook at home."

A situation like this, one that seems to revolve around such an inconsequential practice, can result in substantial amounts of money that are spent, in effect, by default. No one sat down and considered the situation and the alternatives.

How much money is involved in frequent use of the fast-food expedient? A family can easily spend fifty dollars or more a month for the purchase of routine evening meals. That's enough to make real inroads on a debt load. It would also be enough to hire someone to come in twice a month and do some heavy cleaning, which would certainly be one way to help solve the basic problem of getting all the household chores done.

The fast-food expedient is but one example of patterns we can fall into that cost more than we realize and that we perpetuate because the situation hasn't been thought or talked through. Another might include supporting an expensive cross-town commute in the family car for a teenager who has a very ordinary job at some distance from home. Of course, that young person enjoys the use of the car and would rather not give it up. However, it's likely that a similar job can be found closer to home. In such a case, the solution may be to require payment for mileage on the car, which would make the young person weigh the benefits and disadvantages of working closer to home.

There are plenty of other ways in which people get trapped into routine spending that isn't necessary. Some of these may include rituals of entertaining or of relating to others in the family. Do you hold Open House on New Year's Day, even when the enjoyment has faded? Do you host a bridge group because that's what you've always done? Do you call an elderly relative long-distance at a specific time, even when the call could be placed at a less expensive time, such as before 8 A.M.? It's worth checking into any routine that costs money and asking yourself, "Why am I doing this? Could there be a less costly way to achieve the same goal?"

So, spender, know thyself. Watch out for the money traps, large and small. You know about some individual spending patterns that can cost money. You know some of the ways advertising and merchandising can play on your emotions and get you to open your wallet. You have learned about the high costs that may result from faulty communications (even about small things) with the other people in your life. Out of this knowledge you can salvage dollars to put toward the things you value most.

7.

Winning the Shopping Game

ALTHOUGH WE MAY NOT WANT to recognize the fact, most of us aren't good all-around shoppers. One person may be a whiz in the supermarket, and another may take delight in sorting out the relative bargains offered by different insurance policies, but darn few of us know what we're doing in all areas. What's more, we often let our emotions get tangled up in our spending decisions. Our varying abilities and our sometimes conflicting attitudes about shopping can cost us a lot of money.

If you think careful shopping is just a matter of saving pennies and dimes, you're wrong. Buying clothes is one example. If you consider all the unworn clothes hanging in your closets I think you will agree with the experts who say that at least a third of what we buy is not worn or not worn out because of poor choices in color, style, or fit. How important is this? Most families spend at least ten percent of their income for clothing. If your family's annual income is twenty thousand dollars, that means a minimum of six hundred dollars a year may be wasted on poor clothing selection.

Hurried or unwise purchases can add up to a big chunk of useless spending. You can lose money when you buy something that really doesn't suit your purpose or when you buy the right thing but pay more for it than you needed to.

You won't reap the benefits of competent shopping, however,

unless you make up your mind to invest the time and energy it requires. Successful shopping will get easier as you practice the strategies and tactics I explain in this chapter. I also have some further suggestions for conserving dollars. However, your first task in becoming a good shopper is to know a little more about your personal approach to shopping.

SHOPPER, KNOW THYSELF

There was a time a few years ago when I characterized my own shopping style as "unsafe at any speed." While I did well with the groceries and routine necessities, I was no good in any other department. When it came to buying major items for the house, selecting gifts or clothing (most especially clothing), I had two unsuccessful approaches.

One approach was to wait until the purchase could be postponed no longer and then to go out and plunk down money for the first thing I saw that came anywhere near what I wanted. My other approach was to try to remedy this by wandering from store to store keeping an open mind. This translated as not having any plan. I would feel more bewildered and intimidated with every passing minute I spent in those stores. My first approach yielded a houseful of not-quite-right items, usually bought at a higher price than necessary. My second approach accomplished absolutely nothing and made me feel depressed.

You may enjoy shopping, or this may be the last way on earth you want to spend your time. There are some interesting stereotypes involved here. Men are supposed to hate to shop. Women, on the other hand, are perceived as being so fond of shopping that this will be their pet recreation when they accompany their husbands to a business convention, and it is the mode of exploration they are expected to prefer when on vacation and visiting a foreign port.

Well, it ain't necessarily so. If you, as a man, spend lunch hours window shopping and comparing prices on this or that, and if you, as a woman, share my suffering from what was once described as Fear of Saks, you can stop thinking that this is your own private secret. Attitudes toward shopping, and skill at it, know no gender boundaries.

Shopping can be fun, or it can be just one more of life's tedious tasks. In many cases you'll have to delegate responsibility for shopping just as you do for any other chore. The total amount of work should be divided fairly, but the person who is best at doing one thing should take the lead in accomplishing it.

SHOPPING AS RECREATION

It could be that you're one of those people who do enjoy shopping. You are making a mistake, however, if you use shopping too often as recreation. The more time you spend in stores looking at merchandise, the more things you are likely to want to own. Your dollars can slip away if you overuse shopping as a way to pass the time.

If wandering through the halls of commerce has become the way in which you channel your spare energies and your striving for self-esteem, as well as your time on those weekends when there is nothing else to do, you need to rethink your choice of recreation. Relegate shopping to the businesslike role it should have.

EFFICIENT USE OF YOUR TIME AND ENERGY

Shopping calls for a businesslike attitude. It is important to be selective about how you spend your time and energy. You can't go rummaging through back issues of *Consumer Reports* every time you want to buy a can of peas or a roll of cellophane tape. Get in the habit of deciding before you shop how much effort the purchase merits. There are three things you should consider in making this decision.

First, how often do you need to buy this item? You will need separate shopping strategies for items that you rarely buy and for those you purchase over and over again. What about a $2 item that you only have to buy once a year? Just go ahead and get it. You might shop half the town and find it for $1.79, or you might take the first opportunity you see and pay $2.09. The price difference isn't worth the extra fuss.

Suppose, however, that you're shopping for an item that will be a recurring expense. It will definitely pay to find the self-service gas station that consistently gives the most gallons for the fewest dollars. It will also serve you well to find the supermarket with a good track record for low shelf prices. Make some good general decisions and then abide by them as much as you can. Set yourself a pattern for shopping at places where you'll get good buys in things like men's underwear, kids' tennis shoes, groceries, or supplies for the garden. Then go to these places where bargains are generally the best and be done with it. Your time is worth much more than the few dimes gained by hours of supersharp foraging through every store in town or making a career out of redeeming cents-off coupons.

Second, consider the price of the item you're planning to buy. It is, of course, worth your time and energy to shop around for each and every one of those big-ticket items. This *is* the time to check through back issues of *Consumer Reports.* This is also the time to check with people you know who've made a similar purchase. But perhaps the most important thing you can do is get out the telephone directory and follow the Rule of Three. That means making a minimum of three phone calls to check out prices.

I used this tactic recently when I was shopping for a replacement for my old slide projector. Information I got over the phone told me I could buy one specific model of a medium-priced projector for anywhere from $262.00 to $187.46. What's more, I could buy a demonstration model of the same thing for $139.90. My fifteen-minute investment in phone calls therefore offered me the potential of saving $75 on identical new models and an extra $47 if I settled for equipment that had already had a little use. The difference between $262 and roughly $140 is $122. That isn't a bad savings for a quarter of an hour's worth of telephoning.

Here's another idea. Start developing a reference library of sales catalogues. Pick them up whenever you have the chance and keep them together in one convenient place. Whether you're checking out prices on gourmet cooking equipment or shock absorbers for the car, it's handy to have a source of price comparisons.

Third, consider the margin for bargain. What's margin for

bargain? That's the chance that there might be some deviation on the price of any specific item. It's well worth considering even when your purchase does not fall into the big-ticket category.

With some kinds of purchases the margin for bargain will be small no matter what the price. Rock-bottom prices won't vary much with products for which there's a great deal of demand because the prices for such items have usually pretty well sorted themselves out. Suppose, however, that you're shopping for something that's relatively nonstandard. It could be some printed stationery, a particular kind of tropical fern, or maybe some specialized woodworking tools. The price structure you'll encounter may vary enormously.

Here's another example from my experience. I needed some letterhead to use in my work. I checked with a friend who had recently ordered some stationery and got her recommendation. Then I looked in the phone book's yellow pages and found two print shops that were fairly close to my home. I called all three to learn about prices.

I found that while the cost per page was about the same at all the shops, they had differing policies about minimum orders. One shop wouldn't print less than five hundred sheets, and another required a minimum of four hundred. The shop my friend had recommended, however, would take a minimum order of two hundred. I would have had to buy far more stationery than I needed if I hadn't shopped any further than those first two print shops in my neighborhood.

QUALITY CONSIDERATIONS
Salespeople usually try to assure us that we're the sort of person who wants the top-quality item. Whether you're buying a snack food or a soldering iron, you often don't need the extra benefits that go along with best-of-the-line. Here are some examples.

Suppose your youngster has been playing the violin for six years and practicing three hours a day for the past two years. Qualifying play-offs are coming up that will determine whether or not this young person can compete for an eight-thousand-dollar scholarship to a prestigious music school. Now may be the time to invest in a topnotch professional-quality instrument.

Suppose, however, the city Cub Scout play-offs for archery are in the offing. Your nine-year-old has shown a passing interest in the last few months. Do you buy an expensive bow? No, no matter what the salesman has to say. Before you go beyond an investment in learner's equipment, you should wait and see what happens with that young man's interest in archery.

Buying the finest isn't always the most useful idea, but it's almost always useful to be aware of quality distinctions. You may later be uncomfortable with a purchase if it turns out to be of lesser quality than you intended. You'll be particularly vulnerable to this kind of mistake if the family situation you grew up with dictated a none-but-the-cheapest policy. People who've grown up with money tend to be aware of quality differences all up and down the line, but those from less advantaged backgrounds tend to be blind to quality differences they've never sampled.

If, for example, when you were young your experience with restaurants was limited mainly to the local hot dog and hamburger places, you learned little about the quality differences in restaurants that charge higher prices. You might not have made much distinction between a Howard Johnson's meal, the local tourist trap that featured imitation antique fixtures and overpriced steak, or that little French restaurant with the understated decor and meals that would bring rave notices from Julia Child. Your ignorance might not have posed any problem then. However, if you haven't had a chance to educate yourself, you may make a mistake when you have the obligation of taking someone very important out to dinner.

So, there can be problems associated with quality blindness. There's also a solution to this kind of problem. Say you need some clothes to wear to a new job in which you're anxious to create the right image for yourself. You don't want to muff those all-important first impressions. What's more, you don't want to buy the wrong things and later have to buy a work wardrobe all over again.

Here's how to educate yourself about quality differences in

clothes. First, gather up your courage and walk into several of the most expensive stores in your community. Look at what they have to offer. Check the workmanship, the feel of the fabric, and the styling features that seem to be on the leading edge of fashion. Make a mental note of price ranges, but walk out without buying anything.

Next, head straight for the nearest discount house or whatever low-priced emporium you can find. Look at what's offered. What are the hallmarks of cheapness? Again, check the feel and drape of the fabric and the details of workmanship and style. Note prices, too. Finally, repeat the procedure at your local midrange department store.

Now, and only now, are you ready to buy.

Make a decision about the level of quality that will be most appropriate for your circumstances. Make some rough guesses about the prices you'll probably have to pay, and determine how many of which items you can afford. You may want to buy some items at one quality level and some at another. Then go ahead, buying the garments that have the most attributes of the expensive clothing and the fewest characteristics of the cheap merchandise.

Incidentally, when you make your sojourn to those expensive stores, you might want to apply for a charge account at each of them. Why? To get their catalogues and sales brochures. Once you're on the mailing list, you'll have a free supply of fashion and price bulletins. You can't, of course, get the heft and feel of a fine fabric by looking at pictures. Nonetheless, you should be able to pick up a lot of useful ideas. Also, you might consider shopping some of the end-of-season sales at these stores. (You may need to be cautious. If you're uncertain about your sales resistance, leave all your credit cards at home and take only the cash you can afford to spend.)

KNOW-HOW FOR SALE

Now's the time to pull you back from the elegant arena of high-priced stores and ask you to consider a more mundane matter. In many routine purchases we may pay much more than we need to because we're buying know-how along with the merchandise. This merchandising tactic I call the Hamburger Helper Ploy. What it boils down to is this: If you don't know how to put together a dish, they'll sell you the way to do it, along with a few overpriced ingredients.

This ploy is used over and over again in our supermarkets, sometimes with food and sometimes with other items. All of those gravy mixes, boil-in-the-bag vegetables with sauces, fancy salad dressings, and seasoned instant rice concoctions sell the same thing: know-how. They also sell you a lot more salt, sugar, and other ingredients than you may want in your diet.

You can get the know-how much more cheaply out of a cookbook or from someone you know. It wasn't until I was thirty years old that I learned how to make gravy. The lesson took about five minutes. Try measuring that knowledge against, say, another thirty years of using at least a dozen cans a year of fifty-cent gravy or sauce. Even at this minimum rate, that one brief lesson has saved me $180. The ingredients for gravy cost very little.

Let's look at another area in which know-how is sold: household cleaners. Uncertain about how to clean the oven? You need never admit it as long as you buy the expensive product that promises to make the job a breeze. Never had to clean a toilet? Feeling reluctant and worried you'll have to put your hands into the water? Never fear. Someone has the chemical and the contraption that will help you solve the problem in an expensive way.

Here's what one home economist has to say about the cleaning-product situation. "Do you have $50 under your sink?" asks Jane Schoppe of the University of California at Davis. "With spray-on this and miracle-clean that, it's not difficult to spend that much or more on cleaning preparations in a short time."

Schoppe advises making up your own mixtures and buying only a few products — those with multiple uses. She says ammonia, bleach, and detergents can be combined to do most jobs. (Never use ammonia and chlorine bleach together, however, because the resulting fumes can make you sick.)

For that oven-cleaning job, Schoppe suggests putting a saucer with a half cup of ammonia in the oven when it's cool and leaving the oven door closed overnight. The next morning the grease can be removed by using a cloth dampened with a solution of one cup ammonia and two quarts of water. Total cost by my reckoning: about ten cents worth of ammonia. A replacement for those expensive spray-on cleaners? A solution of two tablespoons of ammonia, two tablespoons of dishwashing liquid, and one quart of water. And how about the toilet bowl challenge? Put in a cup of chlorine bleach and let it stand for a half hour. Then scrub with a plain old toilet brush. You can do a lot of cleaning before you ever chalk up a fifty-dollar tab for supplies.

You may have to invest some time in acquiring know-how about cooking, cleaning, and other tasks around the house. However, an investment of a few hours will serve you for the rest of your life.

SALES RESISTANCE

Your first line of defense is to be aware of all those pressures to buy. Your second line of defense is to have a shopping plan and stick to it. Your final defense may be to develop an instinct for when you should pack up your wallet and head in another direction.

The stores will use every trick to entice you to say yes. If you're reluctant to accept that idea, consider even as basic an item as a shopping cart. Did you know that today's cart is roughly thirty percent larger than it was ten years ago? This is because research has shown that many people who shop for food once a week will buy until they fill up the cart.

Did you know that sometimes you go ahead and make a purchase just because you've reached some inner limit of tolerance for the uncertainties of the shopping procedure? Here's how that can happen. Let's say you're out shopping for some new stereo equipment. You've been looking at speakers and tuners and specifications until you're not certain about anything anymore. You're tired, weary of the confusion, and feeling less than good about your own uncertainty. If you're smart, you'll go home at this point.

If you're in the hands of an experienced salesperson, however, you're likely to walk out of the store with just exactly what he or she has decided you're going to buy. Salespeople can tell when the confusion and fatigue have reached the right pitch. This is when they tell you, "Now, if I were in your place, here's the package I'd go for." Great! Someone has made the decision for you and gotten you off the hook. You'll probably buy that decision, along with time payments and a total price tag that's big in proportion to the money you have available and your original intentions.

Watch out for this have-done-with-it tendency. There's more than one way it can rob you of dollars you'd rather spend elsewhere. It's all-important to remember that this tendency can also affect you after you've made a purchase decision. The matter of credit comes up and you take the credit of convenience offered by the seller.

Shop around for credit. This is another place to apply the Rule of Three and get busy on the telephone. Why pay eighteen percent or more on an installment contract when you might have gotten a shares loan at your credit union at about half that rate?

You are the one who knows the most about yourself, and you'll probably develop your own individual style of sales resistance. However, I'll leave you with one final piece of advice. Don't buy if you find yourself thinking any of the following:

* I suppose it really wouldn't pay to fix up the old one.
* It's so pretty.
* This is a once-in-a-lifetime opportunity.
* The payments aren't all that big.
* I'm sick of shopping and my feet hurt.
* You only go around once.
* Everybody's got one.
* It'll keep peace in the family.
* It's just this once.
* I owe it to myself.
* I know I can't afford it, but . . .
* It isn't exactly what I need, but . . .
* Why not?

GOOD MANAGEMENT

You should place a high value on just plain old good management. It involves organization, planning, and order. It *is* extra work — but then you have to work to earn needlessly spent dollars, too. This is another area in which the work load should be shared fairly by everybody in the family.

Here are just a few examples of what can happen when poor management starts to make inroads on your money supply.

* You'll be a loser if you don't take the time to keep tools and home repair supplies in order. Who enjoys spending $2.98 for epoxy cement only to discover that there was already some in that jumble of stuff pushed back on the shelf? Who wants to learn that another can of enamel will have to be bought for that touch-up job in the bathroom because the lid on the original can wasn't put back on properly and the paint has dried out? How about having to buy a whole new set of drawer pulls for the dresser in the kid's bedroom because you can't locate those spares you stashed? For that matter, who wants to spend a half hour just trying to find a pair of pliers?

* You'll pay more money at the dry cleaners if you come home from work or from a dressy occasion and embark on household chores before you've changed clothes. Ditto if clothes aren't properly hung up. Younger members of the family tend to be the worst offenders here, and a cost-sharing system may turn out to be most cost-effective.

* Dollars will go to waste at the grocery store without good management. Food can stack up at the back of the freezer until it's too frostbitten for good eating. Kids can grab a can of tuna off of the shelf when there's some already mixed for sandwiches sitting in the refrigerator. Those teenagers you dispatched to the store with vague instructions to get something for dinner can come back with steak when you had ground beef in mind. How about your discovery that the recesses of your cupboard concealed six packages of gelatin dessert done in by the

ravages of time, along with four opened and stale boxes of breakfast cereal? Did you dash off to the store without a shopping list and return to find that you now have three dozen eggs and an oversupply of dog food, but you'll have to go back and buy milk?

We all slip up once in a while, and I don't want to lecture you about common sins. Nonetheless, there's a lot more than two-bit savings involved in good management. If your family is living in a disorderly house, a lot of money that could be put to useful purposes will wander off into oblivion.

Why not set up Operation Dollar Salvage and get the whole family involved? You've learned how to do a monthly audit, so you should be able to set up some kind of estimate of how much money has been used for routine expenses. Why not begin a system of competing with your past habits to see how much money your family can earn through good shopping strategies and tactics, sales resistance, and careful management? Then you can embark together on the delicious task of deciding how to use those dollars.

ONE FINAL WORD: FRUGALITY

About now might be the time that you're receptive to a consideration of the joys of frugality. I'm not intending to describe a mean and miserly attitude of pinch-penny denial. I'm thinking instead of an inquiring frame of mind and of freedom of choice. In how many ways, large or small, can you elect to conserve your money for the things you want most?

It's a matter of fact that Americans have forgotten much of the technology of frugality. If you've grown up in recent decades, you've lived in an antifrugal atmosphere. It's only been in recent years that we've started to turn back to some of the principles of conservation that our grandparents knew so well.

"The truth is that during the nation's rush to mid-century prosperity the notion of individual frugality went out of business," said Frank Trippett in a *Time* magazine essay (March 3, 1980). " 'Waste not, want not' has persisted only as a saying, and most people have fallen out of the habit of taking it seriously."

Trippett pointed out that we are at last coming back to a conservation ethic. We're opting for smaller cars, energy savings in the home, vegetable gardens, garage sales, and second-hand shops. "Most Americans once practiced frugality as though it were instinctive, or even religious," Trippett said. "The old ways may even come as an amazement to younger Americans who grew up during the virtually invulnerable affluence that followed World War II."

I remember more frugal times. These were the World War II days of my childhood. Patriotic posters lectured us all: "Use it up. Wear it out. Make it do."

I remember the bread wrappers recycled for lunch-box sandwiches, the tubs of hot sudsy water in the old wringer washer that served first for the sheets and towels and relatively clean items and later for heavily soiled work shirts and pants. I remember the carcass of Sunday's roast chicken going into the pot for a fragrant soup, and the worn-out shirts and pajamas cut up into household wipes and "nose blowers." I remember having the honor of using the old sewing machine to piece together strips of discarded fabric that were then braided and sewn into rag rugs. What's more, I remember winter mornings when I had to get out of a warm bed and could step on those rag rugs instead of the cold linoleum floor.

Why not update the conservation ethic? It can be turned into a lot of fun. If it's a craft project that's needed at your house, why not forgo the expensive precut makings for a hooked rug? Instead, try reviving the lost art of braided rugs. If children need something to do, why not set them to work cutting up paper that's been printed on only one side and stapling the pieces into note pads? Why not explore in your vicinity for fruit or berries that are going to waste and make a social occasion of putting them up? It's nice to have homemade jam to use as a hostess gift instead of a bottle of wine or some expensive candy.

One reason that frugality has been neglected is that many of us have forgotten how. Often we simply don't think of the more frugal options. There's another reason, too. While some kinds of frugality are as quick and easy as more wasteful ways, others do take extra time and effort, as well as imagination. However, the pursuit of frugality can be turned into fun. It can certainly be a great deal more fun than watching reruns of dull television programs. It can also be a lot easier on your finances than using shopping as recreation.

8.

Trouble Spots
and Transitions

T HERE ARE some situations in life that seem to be just
tailor-made for using up money — and often for using it in
ways that don't bring satisfaction. How can you tell when you're
about to get involved in one of these situations? Try looking
over these things you may hear said. See how many you can link
with a potential for using money unwisely.

"Mom and Dad, guess what! Joe and I are going to get married!"

"The stroke was a severe one, and the doctor thinks it's only
a matter of days."

"Congratulations! Your Mom and I have waited for years to
see you hang out your shingle."

"I want a divorce."

"Look, don't hassle me. Jobs will be a lot easier to find at the
end of summer."

"I don't like all those math and science courses, and I don't
need them to graduate."

"Wow! The appraiser just called. He says that old painting is
worth thousands of dollars."

"So you've finally made the decision to retire. Bet you're
really going to live it up now!"

You may recognize the financial implications of some of these
situations but not of others. However, each and every one of
them can bring financial woes. Here's what I've learned about

some of the ways money troubles can develop at times of emotion or of transition, often with more impact than anyone might expect.

WEDDING AND FUNERAL WOES

Not long ago my husband and I attended one of his class reunions. I took the opportunity to talk with people I met there about ways they had spent money. I asked them about spending that, in retrospect, they knew had been unwise. The most typical response went something like this:

"It was our daughter's wedding. When I was a girl, I used to dream of the big wedding I would have, but we had to settle for a very small ceremony. So for my daughter we went all out for a big affair and a reception. Seven months later they split, and we were still paying off the loan!"

When we are faced with a wedding or a funeral, or when a serious illness strikes, we feel pressured (or pressure ourselves) to respond in ways that may not be in keeping with the money we have available. We have been schooled to believe that at such times we can't think about money. We let spending get entangled with our attempts to demonstrate our feelings, even when we know that dollars do not measure love.

Financial counselor William Buckner knows about wedding and funeral bankruptcy. He's seen a number of cases that have put near-fatal strains on a family's finances.

"This is one of those financial traps that seems to catch people regardless of their income," he says. "It's the most difficult, of course, for families with the fewest resources. It always astonishes me to learn that people in the midst of severe debt troubles will take on impossible obligations."

The happier occasions, such as weddings and graduations, are the easier ones to cope with — easier still if you have an open and affectionate relationship with the people involved. Good communication may turn up the information that a young couple isn't putting a high priority on going through the paces of an elaborate wedding ceremony, for instance. Or if a big wedding is what's wanted, ways can be found for a compromise, postponement, or shared expenses. This can save a lot of resentment, as well as money that may be needed elsewhere.

The sad occasions are the really tough ones to cope with. "People seem to feel even less restraint if someone has died or is quite ill," Buckner notes. "They drop everything, make reservations, and take off halfway across the country on a trip they can in no way afford."

I've seen this happen even when the individuals involved have never had a close relationship. I think that spending such as this may correlate to our feelings about the person who is ill or has died. It may be that love triggers such responses, but it may also be frustration about a relationship that has not worked well. What can you do when the world tells you to disregard money?

These situations, too, will be easier if you've made the effort to keep up relationships. By all means talk over future funeral arrangements with people in your family. Also, if you know someone who is ill and dying, gather up your courage and write to him or her before it's too late. If you take the time to tell someone what importance he or she has had in your life and what you remember most fondly about the relationship, your letter will mean much more to you and to that person's family than any costly rememberance sent at the time of the funeral. Homegrown flowers and homemade gifts, even simple letters or phone calls, can be far more eloquent than anything the merchandisers sell.

What about people you genuinely don't like? Nearly all of us know and try to avoid that individual with a personality like cobra venom, or that relative who is a self-centered, self-pitying bore. You needn't forget such a person altogether on important occasions. However, don't turn yourself inside out financially. Omit the grand gesture or the expensive trip. Such measures, after all, are not likely to impress anyone except you. Don't forget, too, that you may be tempted to use a crisis as an antidote to boredom or for relief from coping with your other problems.

THE I'VE-ARRIVED SYNDROME

Let me tell you how this money trap ensnared one young couple I know.

She had worked as a secretary while he went to medical

school. When he started his residency, she started her first pregnancy. They lived in a modest rental home for a while but indulged in some new stereo equipment and some expensive camera gear.

Throughout most of his residency, she struggled valiantly with one car and their conflicting time schedules. About the time he was ready to set up a practice of his own, she declared an end to the car struggle. They became a two-car family during the same month they moved into a new home in a more prestigious neighborhood.

Their mortgage and car payments had to come out of an income reduced by large payments for new office equipment. The end of his first year of practice coincided with a reduction in payments on office equipment, so in the following six months they added a boat for water skiing and a hot tub to their obligations, along with some really stylish clothes. Every lender in town was eager to provide credit on the basis of his M.D.

Then, however, he took a six-week leave from his practice to volunteer his medical services in Southeast Asia. They returned from a celebration of his arrival home to realize they didn't have enough cash to pay the woman hired to mind the baby and the house. Frantic, they began an inventory of finances. They found that when all of their payments and obligations were deducted from his monthly average income, they were left with only two hundred dollars per month for groceries and other routine expenses.

"For years I've looked forward to all the good things that went with being a doctor's wife," the young woman told me. "Now I can't even afford to get my hair cut."

The I've-Arrived money trap waits for anyone who has toiled for years getting through college, setting up a professional practice, or perhaps starting a business. Whatever the event, some line of demarcation is passed, and someone decides that this symbolic event marks the end of struggle and the beginning of prosperity.

The problems emerge because enthusiasm overtakes reality. Feelings of prosperity may derive more from a notion of what now should be attainable than from actual income. This is the time for splurges — eating dinners out, joining the country club, buying another car, or just generally enjoying the good life. The new achievers are likely to move to nicer quarters, take on a big mortgage, and relegate scrimp and make-do to the past.

The situation has been repeated hundreds of times in infinite variations. A college graduate who has just landed a first job may assume a fancy apartment and a new car are easily affordable. A young couple may assume that marriage automatically brings with it enough money to afford all the household equipment they think they should have, right down to deepfreezes and expensive furniture. Anyone newly arrived in a profession that traditionally has been associated with affluence may feel that it's time to cut the parsimony strings and indulge after a long spell of doing without.

What they all have in common is a hazy expectation that everything is affordable. What they need is a brass-tacks session about dollars and cents to figure out the exact consequences of total expenditures on income and their effect on future choices. This is an avoidable money trap — but only if you've got some inkling that you'd best watch out for it. For many people, it's a painful surprise.

MARITAL DISPUTES AND DIVORCE

If I had to name one event in life that's likely to be the most costly, I'd have to say it's divorce. Often, the money starts going in useless directions long before the divorce action erupts. According to marriage counselor Herbert Harris, money can be used in many ways by people who aren't getting along. He explains that a man can spend money away from home as an expression of hostility, or a woman can go on spending sprees in an attempt to compensate for the lack of closeness in a relationship.

When a marriage comes apart at the seams, the individuals face a dual possibility for financial problems. First comes the simple fact that two households are more expensive to maintain than one. It is likely that neither partner will be able to enjoy the standard of living they could afford together, although it may take some time for each to discover the realities of the financial situation. The other possibility for financial trouble stems from the fact that each party in a dissolving marriage may attempt to punish the other by spending money. One lawyer I talked with commented that it is nearly impossible to restrain a determined partner from reckless spending before a property settlement is reached.

"Suppose it's the man who can get his hands on the assets during this interim period," he said. "He can go on flings, buy foolishly, take trips, or whatever. When the time of reckoning comes, he can simply say, 'I was emotionally upset and didn't really know what I was doing.' There's no recourse. The assets to be divided will be just that much smaller."

A woman can overspend, too, by charging a great variety of things to the joint charge accounts before her name has been taken off of them. Once in a while, the situation is reversed, and it's the man who spends while the credit lasts. The individuals involved in such a situation should inform creditors about what is happening and ask them to wait. Joint debts should be taken into account at the time of the final property settlement.

There's no real remedy for the problem of debts that arise out of conflict, unless a couple can agree to disagree in a constructive fashion. The only other recourse is to move as rapidly as possible toward separate finances and the final property settlement.

Even when a marriage has been legally ended the financial battle can go on if the couple engages in a competition to see who can spend the most on the kids. The classic situation is that the mother is left with the role of "meanie," seeing to it that children do their chores and their homework and cope with all of the responsibilities of daily life, while the father takes the role of munificent spender.

He may provide outings and perhaps some outrageous gifts. Usually the heavy spender in such situations soon comes to want a more even-handed relationship with the children and a more meaningful one — or simply runs out of money. At least in circumstances such as these the finances are relatively separate, and each spender must face the consequences of his or her own expenditures. (A note: Grandparents in divorce cases can also involve themselves in spending contests. Some may never come to the realization that dollars do not measure love.)

KIDS WHO WON'T GROW UP

Here are two typical complaints from families who've tried unsuccessfully to cope with such problems.

"When George graduated from high school, we knew he wasn't headed for college. He'd been wanting a certain kind of truck, so that's what we bought him for graduation. It was more than we could easily afford, but we wanted him to have good transportation so that this wouldn't be a problem when he looked for work. Well, that darn truck made a lot more trips to the beach than to any job interviews. He's worked here and there a little bit, but right now his truck is up on blocks in the driveway because he can't afford repairs, and George is in the house flat on his back watching television."

"Marsha started at our community college after high school, but she was running with a crowd we didn't like. We talked her into going to a private college out of town. It's run by our church and is very strict. We're in hock up to our eyeballs trying to pay the board and tuition bills. She didn't apply herself to her studies, and she just played around for a while. Now we've learned that she has gotten herself kicked out for some silly stunt."

Marriage counselor Herbert Harris offers some insight into this type of circumstance. "Many middle-class kids have underachieved, and they will just take the long route in getting to maturity," he told me. "In fact, a majority of those teenagers in the troubled category will continue to have problems in early adulthood. There may be indebtedness, and also disruptions in their marriages if they marry early. They may throw away money and time, and possibly become absentee parents. They may be poor workers, trying to see how they can get by with the least responsibility. These young people can come from stable, successful families, too."

Money often goes in useless directions when a family is faced with the problem of a son or daughter who just won't grow up. Some kids resist with great ingenuity all efforts to see that they learn to give as well as get, to find a job with good prospects, or to embark on schooling that gives any promise of making them economically self-sufficient.

What can parents do?

"Working on the relationship is a better investment than adding extra money for equipment or schools," Harris says. "People may tend to have too much faith in outside influences, such as private or parochial schools. Firm direction by parents, and open discussion about what's going on, may be a better option."

In my own experience, I've seen parents who are making mistakes or who lack direction in their own lives let their problems spill over and block the growing up process in their children. I've also seen youngsters in similar situations grow up to be fine people.

I've watched thoughtful parents who do everything right end up with fine offspring or with awful messes. All situations in which kids refuse to grow up are heartbreaking, but this last circumstance is perhaps the hardest to cope with.

Whatever the situation in your family, you'll be up against some hard decisions if one of your sons or daughters is taking the long route to maturity. There may be times when a money investment — a working wardrobe, a good used car, some money for school — is just the ticket. But I'd recommend a hard line and no largess based on unfounded hopes. It's seldom that an unearned expenditure will somehow work the magic necessary to transform a loafer into an achiever. A quid pro quo agreement may be necessary, or perhaps an understanding that the youngster must first come up with "matching funds." These can be earned with any kind of stopgap work.

You can't use money in the hope that it alone will solve problems with children who resist becoming adults. You may have to resign yourself to the possibility that your son or daughter may make a great number of mistakes. Letting young people face the consequences of their own mistakes can often be the most constructive course of action open to you.

COLLEGE THAT GOES NOWHERE

The college money trap — investment in an education that probably won't produce substantial income benefits — is still a common one. In our culture, white males are most often steered into the kind of education that will reap financial rewards. Women and minorities, particularly non-Asian minorities, more often go into the "soft" fields.

According to University of California statistics, women and non-Asian minorities commonly lack the high school preparation in math and laboratory science that will allow them to move easily into the first-year technical courses required for many fields. Without these basic courses, the only fields open will be the "helping professions" and law or journalism, all of which are overcrowded.

It's very easy for a young student or for a re-entry woman to take the path of greatest familiarity and least resistance and opt for one of the lower-paying fields. I'm not trying to knock the intrinsic value of a liberal arts education. However, if earning capacity is important (and it nearly always is) appropriate measures must be taken to achieve it. Many college graduates plugging away at monotonous low-paying jobs are all too familiar with this harsh truth. There are few ways to turn a B.A. in art history or a specialization in seventeenth-century literature into solid money-earning capacity.

Despite all the talk in the last decade about the declining market value of college degrees in humanities and liberal arts, many people embark on college educations with little regard for the economic outcome. Psychology professor Henry Lindgren has undertaken some research on the attitudes of college students about earning money. He reports that many students are still unrealistic about the role that money and other economic factors play in the real world.

"Students may go to elaborate lengths to deny any suggestion that the money motive plays a part in their lives," he told me. "This rigid position has melted somewhat in the last year or so . . . but students still flock into courses that will prepare them for careers in social work, the creative arts, family counseling,

clinical psychology, and education. The unemployment and un-
der-employment which plague these fields do not seem to deter
them."

National statistics back up Lindgren's view. In just one field,
teacher preparation, figures from the National Education Association show that the number of graduates seeking teaching
positions in 1979 greatly exceeded the number of jobs available.
In that year 135,500 graduates were looking for teaching positions, but there were only 74,750 jobs available nationwide.
Nearly half of the graduates couldn't find work in their chosen
profession.

If you're providing for someone's college education, or if
you're going to go back and seek to finish one for yourself,
there's only one rule that makes sense. If you want to have
wage-earning capacity, plan to get it. A college degree, just any
degree, won't guarantee it, no matter how appealing the sales
talk from the chairman of the Humanities Department. He or
she, after all, is in the same position as the people who sell
advertising. Earning a living is essential.

SUDDEN WEALTH

Let's say you discover that the tarnished thing Aunt Tillie gave
you so long ago is solid silver, antique, and worth a bundle. Or
you win a lottery, or a lawsuit, or come into money because a
relative died. Could this possibly be bad news? Yes!

Consider what happened with one couple. Tim and Lisa
Smith are in their late fifties. Tim had cancer, a tumor that the
medical people provided by his health insurance told him was
inoperable. Tim and Lisa immediately set out on a search for a
better option. They found it at a prestigious private clinic. The
"inoperable" cancer was removed in a difficult and hazardous
operation, and Tim is now well on the road to recovery.

As soon as possible Tim and Lisa were on their way to a
lawyer's office to sue the original health provider not only for
the cost of Tim's life-saving surgery but also for mental anguish
and an assortment of other damages. So far this is a story with
a happy ending. The lawsuit has yet to be tried, but Tim's
lawyer is promising a prompt and successful outcome.

On the strength of this, however, the Smiths have already agreed to buy an expensive car to take a celebration trip across the country. Was this their idea? No, it was the idea of a rather pushy friend, who has also persuaded them to take a "deal" on her used Mercedes — at what seemed to me to be a high price.

This friend isn't the only one with an interest in their new financial prospects. There's a former classmate who wants Tim to invest in his new business and a nephew who wants a little help to go to law school. Not everybody wants something for himself. Lisa has a friend who is just dying to help her pick out a new wardrobe and another who is standing by with advice on how to redecorate their house. The Smiths, who are reluctant to hurt anyone's feelings, are likely to see even more erosion of the money they expect to get before they learn how to say no.

If you're suddenly "in the money," you'll discover that it's a struggle not only to keep your hands on it but also to make your own decisions about what to do with it. You're going to be in particular trouble if the discrepancy between your newfound wealth and the financial situation of your friends and associates is especially large.

Professor Henry Lindgren points out that among low-income people the big winner is likely to become an abnormal person to his friends and neighbors. Here's what most often happens, according to Lindgren. "First the newly wealthy person must invite everybody to a 'big party,' " he told me, "and then he must distribute the rest in gifts and 'loans.' "

While this tendency is more obvious among people who have little money, you may be in for a share of it from at least some of the people you know. We do inherit attitudes about money, and some of our families come from low-income backgrounds. The pressure to get the money spent and return to the same status as everybody else is likely to emerge in one form or another.

In his book *Great Expectations: The Psychology of Money* (published by William Kaufmann, Inc., 1980), Lindgren cites the extreme example of a woman who lived in one of the worst slums of Rio de Janeiro. She had kept a diary of sorts of her life as a prostitute. A news reporter who made her acquaintance helped her write a book about her experiences, a book that became a best seller.

When the money started to come in, Lindgren reports, she did not move quickly enough in leaving her surroundings. Her neighbors learned of her wealth. "As she and her hired helpers tried to move her meager belongings out of her shack," he relates, "her erstwhile friends pelted them with stones and garbage, shouting curses and imprecations."

If you come into money your neighbors surely aren't going to start throwing garbage and shouting curses. It could be, however, that people around you will feel some traces of hostility toward sudden wealth if it is not immediately shared. If you come into money you may discover friends, relatives, and neighbors who want you to throw a party, loan them money, or build a swimming pool they can use. I'm not saying all windfall money should go directly into conservative investments and stay there. Some kind of marvelous splurge may be the wisest use you can make of it. However, you should be sure you do your own deciding. Don't yield to pressure about how your money should be used.

ADJUSTING TO RETIREMENT

There's one more money trap waiting for you later in life. You may fall into some unwise spending patterns as you make that transition into retirement. Financial mistakes have been made even by those people who have anticipated for years the dollars and cents they will need for their leisure years. This is because people often don't really think through what they will do with that leisure.

Here's one example, the story of a busy and seemingly happy couple who hit emotional and financial trouble within months after they entered retirement. He had been an executive. He was reluctant to admit it, but he did not want to leave behind him his satisfying world — the expense accounts, the business entertaining and travel, the secretaries and subordinates. His wife had been just as busy, with an active circle of her own and a great deal of independence.

They had made no specific plans but followed a whim and the urgings of a salesman for recreational vehicles. They bought a luxury model and set out to tour the country. They had thought in terms of a three-month trip, but within weeks the enforced isolation and intimacy had them at each other's throats. They managed to return home with their marriage intact and immediately put the travel rig up for sale. They found they had to settle for far less than what they had paid for it.

Not all couples can as easily afford such a mistake, but the experience of these two people has been repeated in infinite variations by a great number of retirees.

"Retirement is roughest for men who have worked all their lives and had no outside interests," Kathie Lefler, a retirement benefits counselor at the University of California, told me. According to Lefler, retirement — and how one will fill up all those empty hours — can be a fearsome subject for many prospective retirees.

"Among many people who fear retirement, there is a refusal to think about it or to talk over possible alternatives," she says. "What we try to do at preretirement meetings is provide a starting point for people to talk about it." She reports that at these retirement meetings she asks husbands and wives to fill out questionnaires without discussing their responses with each other. One page of the form, according to Lefler, deals with whether the couple will relocate. The page happens to be arranged with the top half to be filled out if the couple will relocate and the bottom half if they will remain in the same home.

"Many times I've seen one spouse filling out the top half of the page and the other the bottom. They just haven't talked to each other about it," she says.

The experiences of the retirees that Lefler has worked with, as well as the experience of others, point to some definite guides for moving into retirement happily and without pointless use of money or unwarranted hardship. First and foremost, obviously, is the need to find some way to talk over expectations about lifestyle and how time and money will be spent.

If a man has devoted his life to his career and not developed outside hobbies or nonwork interests, part-time work, consulting, or perhaps volunteer work in a field that welcomes his particular skills can provide an excellent transition.

The lifestyle that will be required by a reduced income should be sampled. The easiest way is simply to start setting aside the difference between working and retirement income. This can produce some delightful dividends a few years down the road, too, should you want an expensive trip or some other kind of special splurge.

Don't assume that hunting and fishing vacations, or whatever form of complete escape from work responsibilities you prefer, represent what you would most like to do on a regular basis. Think twice, for instance, about moving to that remote mountain lake. When on-the-job pressures no longer exist, you may discover other ways you prefer to use your time. What's more, you may discover it's extremely difficult to live in a scenic hideaway when ordinary shopping or a visit to the dentist requires a forty-mile trip.

Finally, don't get into a business venture that will restrict your freedom unless you know what you are undertaking. Many people harbor dreams of a small retail store, a motel, or perhaps a dairy farm, with no realistic understanding of the day-to-day year-round responsibilities.

Whatever choices you make when you retire, you will need the same skills for on-target spending that you've always needed. These, along with some good means for sharing ideas about what you genuinely want and don't want, become even more important in a retirement situation.

* * *

Life's trouble spots and transitions can extend from graduation to retirement — and then keep right on happening. There will always be times when you face a situation in which money flows like arterial bleeding — in spurts. However, there are some generalizations we can make about these times and courses of action we can take to alleviate financial disruption.

Here are the generalizations:

* There's usually more than just one person, or just one couple, involved.
* Rigid thinking about what *ought* to be done governs at least one person's actions.
* Good communication can avoid a lot of needless spending, but there will always be some things or some people that can't be changed. You will just have to live with them.

And there are some universal rules to apply in dealing with possible spending outbursts:

* Make your own choices; don't let other people or outside circumstances unduly sway your thinking.
* Look for the widest possible range of options. You're not obliged to demonstrate love with dollars, and you can set your own terms when dealing with dictatorial people.
* Make sure you're not overresponding to a situation just because you feel something must be done immediately, because your life seems dull or unrewarding, or because there is something in the situation that makes you feel guilty.

Whatever the situation, you're not obliged to follow what seems to be the conventional pattern of spending, although you may choose to do this. Self-direction and unfettered thinking can serve you well.

PART III

How to Spend

Happily Ever After

9.

Getting Your Spending Picture Into Clear Focus

VERY FEW PEOPLE know exactly what they want to do. I remember reading once, years ago, of one woman who did. She was a person of very limited means, and her grand passion was traveling on cruise ships. I think of her as the "ship lady." At the time she was interviewed for the article I read, she had for a number of years been devoting all of her available time and money to traveling. She had gone by ship to nearly every part of the world.

How did she accomplish this? The ship lady held a low-paying job but had no one to provide for other than herself. Most of the year, when she wasn't traveling, she lived in a small room. She spent no money she did not absolutely have to. She spoke of always buying the cheapest food and of searching out overripe produce at bargain prices. She said she wore one tweed suit almost constantly and always went without stockings because they were too expensive to replace. She also spoke at great length, of course, of the joy she derived from her annual travels and of the many places she had seen and the people she had met.

I doubt that you or I would want to emulate the ship lady. We want more than one outfit to wear, and we wouldn't want to be obliged to cut away the rotten parts of potatoes every time we fixed dinner. We don't want a one-dimensional life. Most of us have other people to consider, and we prefer variety. It's the rare person who knows exactly what he or she wants and a rarer one yet whose needs and wants don't change over time.

How clearly focused are your spending priorities?

As you worked through the first section of this book, you probably came to a fairly good understanding of those priorities. The purpose of this chapter is to help you refine that understanding. We'll review your spending priorities. I'll give you a structured way to identify spending mistakes you may be making. Finally, I'll show you how to check your spending against your goals to find out if your money has gone for what you've been saying is important. This is what I call the Congruence Test.

The ship lady could certainly pass the Congruence Test with flying colors. She said what she wanted most was ocean travel, and that's exactly the goal to which she turned every resource she could muster. You're not likely to find any such clearcut picture when you examine your own spending. Most people don't.

Let's consider what happened with one person who has tried out my ideas. She's Debra L., a thirty-year-old technical editor who has recently been promoted to an administrative position. One of her major goals has been to live in San Francisco. Only last year she managed to make the transition from her East Coast home to her new job in California, and she's living in downtown San Francisco. She's delighted to be there, despite a fifty-mile commute each way to her job.

"If it ever came to a choice of changing my job or changing where I live, the job would have to go," she says.

Certainly, there's no problem so far with the Congruence Test for Debra. She does feel, however, that she has problems with how she spends money. "I'm earning more than my father ever did, but I still have trouble making ends meet," she says. That's why she was willing to try out my ideas.

Let's look at what she put down as her fondest ambitions and what she's done with her time and money in the past. Remember, back in Chapter Two I asked you to list some things you'd dreamed of doing? I asked Debra to do the same thing. Of course, by this time, as she was already living in San Francisco,

she had just taken this goal off her wish list. Here's her first
ten-item dream list.

WHAT I DREAM OF

---

1. Time and money to travel throughout the U.S.

2. An apartment full of modern furniture I love.

3. Clothes that I'd feel beautiful in.

4. A house on a hill with a wonderfully large yard.

5. A bookstore of my own—for the books, not the business.

6. Theater and concert tickets for absolutely everything.

7. Time and money for vacations, vacations, vacations.

8. An unstructured life (not an 8–5 job) and more leisure.

9. Ability to travel home (Boston) whenever I wished.

10. Buy a beautiful car—a BMW.

Let's look at what happened when Debra redid that first
dream list according to the four categories: Security, Caring for
Others, Buyables, and Leisure.

"I think I was ahead of you on one part," she told me. "I knew
what I wanted to do with my leisure time. But I had to really
think about the Security part. I knew I wanted to help take care
of my parents." When Debra thought through the Security
section, she had some items that weren't on her dream list but
were certainly on her mind: Medical benefits and financial security for her parents, and a comfortable place for them to live
from which they would not have to move. For herself she added
that she wanted to go back to college and get an M.B.A. because
of the better job opportunities it would provide.

"At thirty, I still haven't given much thought to retirement
nor have I thought seriously about investing because the money

isn't available," she says. (Spending plans that she drew up later show specific amounts allocated for her parents, but she's still deferring additional investments.)

What about the Caring for Others category? Debra's altruistic instincts included a wish to help feed starving people, see that poor children have equal social and cultural opportunities, and also a desire that Israel would continue to exist.

"This is the Social Welfare major in me coming to the surface," she observed. "When I thought about these some more, I realized that I would have to be less global. I'm starting to learn to think in smaller terms — of local things where I'll be able to make a more direct impact."

How about Buyables? When she remade her list she added a few more specific items. A trip throughout the U.S.A., a visit to Boston, perhaps a vacation in London. Then she added a sapphire or emerald ring. She specified "beautiful clothes with someone's name on them, even if this is gauche." She retained her wish for a BMW, and added paintings for the bare walls of her apartment, a large modern kitchen "with all appliances and gadgets," including a washing machine, dryer, dishwasher, and "sheets, pillowcases, towels, bathroom stuff galore."

As for Leisure, Debra had included in her original dream list time and money to travel, books, an unstructured life, and theater tickets "for absolutely everything." When asked to expand on this she also included time to share with friends and family and "a new love," visits to museums of art and science, and time "to enjoy San Francisco when there are no tourists." Another important goal was "time for *me* — to be quiet with no work pressures." She also specified classes in history and English, psychology and sociology, and a Master's degree in college and community counseling, "just for enjoyment." She wanted someone to clean her apartment and do her laundry. Finally she included "a massage whenever I want — professional or otherwise — and a facial by experts."

After finishing her comprehensive lists, Debra got right down to everyday practicalities and did her first Monthly Audit and Worksheet for Six-Month Planning. That first audit showed cash outlays of $480 — "more than I had expected" — and an installment payment total of $155, with interest of $31. "I knew I was spending a lot in interest," she says, "but this was the first time I really had to add it all up."

When she filled out her first Worksheet for Six-Month Planning, Debra did a good job of including priorities from her lists. What's more, as she followed the format from Chapter Four and went through the roots review, she found some items she labeled "Aha!"

Here's how her Worksheet for Six-Month Planning looked.

ITEM	ROOTS REVIEW	SUBSTITUTION	TIMING
Trip to Boston	OK	—	2 months
Coffee table	Aha!	—	—
Bookcase	OK	—	4 months
Time for friends	OK	—	Now
Paintings	OK	Paint wall?	4 months
Theater tickets	OK	Some, not all	Now
Someone to clean my apartment	OK	—	Later
Financial help for parents	OK/Aha!	Talk to others	Now + 3 months+ 6 months
Trip to Oregon to visit friends	OK	—	3 months

Debra said that the thinking she did for the Roots Review and for Substitutions gave her some new ideas. "It was very interesting to go over the influence my parents' style may have had on my spending," she says. "They always had a 'never enough' style and wouldn't use credit."

She remembered that the family invariably did without until the cash was in hand. Then purchases were made. "The first thing I did when I was on my own was to get a credit card and buy a recliner," she says. "I remember that wonderful feeling of freedom. I just went out and got what I wanted. Of course, I was careful after that and paid off the chair before I bought other things, but the freedom was wonderful."

Debra reported another insight.

"I had been planning to buy a coffee table, but I realized it wasn't something I really wanted. I didn't even think about not having one until a man I'm dating commented (the first time he was in my apartment) that I didn't have a coffee table." She had been trying to set aside money to buy one and was delighted that she no longer felt obligated to do so.

What else did Debra discover?

"When it came to providing for my parents, I didn't think about anyone else in the family taking any responsibility," she said. "Nonetheless, I'm going to talk to the others about this. But while I don't see why our parents should be my sole responsibility, I have to admit this feeling comes from within me, not from my parents or anyone else."

I suspect that before Debra finishes the conversations with others in her family about responsibility for her parents, she will also have to find out from them what they want and need.

Nonetheless, even before she gained all of these new insights and made minor changes in her financial planning, Debra's use of money in relation to what she's written on the lists of what she wants gives her a good score on the Congruence Test. She is doing what she set out to do — live in San Francisco and enjoy the benefits that go with an urban life.

How about you?

You're not likely to find an altogether clear-cut picture when you compare your fondest dreams to your actual spending. Few of us do. And for many of us, the ways in which money is spent represents a compendium of the wants and needs of several people. We'll deal in the next chapter with the tactics for including everybody's wishes in an all-family spending list, but right now let's concentrate on getting your own spending and priorities into sharp, clear focus.

It's easy to find out in detail whether you're matching your actual spending to your objectives. We'll do this with a six-month analysis of your spending. The first part of this analysis will document the amounts you've spent. The second part will review the choices you've made about what to do with money.

The information for this six-month review will come from your monthly bank statements, your cancelled checks, and the itemized charge statements that came with your bank card and department store bills.

When you read these instructions, the entire process may sound like a lot of work to you, but it's actually easy — and fascinating. Many people who've tested it for me say they finish in an hour or so. More important, they report they're really able to make use of the information they turn up.

On the next page is the worksheet to use in Step One of your Six-Month Analysis so that you can determine the amounts of money you've spent. You'll be using the same procedure that you used for the Monthly Audit in Chapter Four. This worksheet, too, should be added to your notebook.

Going down the left side of this worksheet for Step One are spaces for six months. List your most recent month first, that month for which you did an audit when you were working on Chapter Four. Then add the names of each month going backward in time. Use the names of the months, rather than numbers, to avoid confusion as you refer back to each preceding bank statement.

For the first month just copy in the totals from the audit you've already done. For each preceding month, follow the Monthly Audit procedure and recreate the information as best you can. Fill in the totals for Cash so that they include groceries and pocket money. Fill in the totals of everything else paid by . check; this gives you the Not-Cash total. Then fill in the infor-

SIX-MONTH ANALYSIS: STEP ONE

Month	Cash Total	Not-Cash Total	Installments	Interest	Debt
————					
————					
————					
————					
————					

mation about your installment debts — total paid, total interest, and total still due.

You now have a general picture of the amounts of money you've spent; those totals that can be used to help understand your spending. You've finished Step One.

Debra reported that she found some surprises. She's also decided to start keeping closer track of where her money goes.

"There were several months in which I was spending more than I made," she says. "Not by charging things — just that the cash and other outgo was more than income." She worried about how this could happen. "I guess my cash flow is just uneven, but I'd like to understand it better," she says.

Debra was also surprised at the amount she was spending in cash. "I thought I was spending more for groceries, but I've decided it must more often be for eating in restaurants or going places."

Debra had never kept track of what she'd spent, except for records she keeps of her car expenses. "I think I'm going to start keeping records of what I spend, at least most of it," she said. "How can I spend $400 and not know where the cash goes?"

How about you?

What might you learn from this first part of the Six-Month Analysis? I'm sure you'll get some insights, just as Debra did, but I'll also ask you to look specifically for some things. To begin with, are you practicing brinksmanship? Of course, if you're heavily involved in this money trap, you're already painfully aware of it; however, you may not be aware of it if you've simply been sliding gently in that direction. If your interest payments and installment debt outstanding have been creeping up in recent months, you'll have to consider putting a higher priority on getting your spending in better balance with your income.

What else can you do? Look at the installment total for each month and the total of all installments debts you owe. This will give you an idea of the actual interest you've been paying — the stated interest plus any minimums or carrying costs. You may want to find a way to reduce these amounts.

One solution is to increase your monthly payments. Or you can always go to your credit union or bank for a lower-cost loan and pay that off instead of using the costly bank-card or department-store loans. Watch out, however, for the temptation to take on new installment obligations while you're still paying off that lower-rate loan! Another tactic is to pay off smaller debts as rapidly as possible so there'll be fewer accounts on which to pay service charges.

You may discover one other thing from the analysis of the amounts of money you've been spending: whether or not there are Up-Down patterns to your spending. If you are given to ups and downs that influence your spending, you probably already know it. Nonetheless, this is a checkpoint time to review for that sort of pattern, one more chance to remind yourself that you may need to substitute some other form of gratification for impulsive spending and find some other way to boost your morale or express your exuberance.

Now you're ready to go on to the second part of your Six-Month Analysis. In Step Two you're going to look at some of the specific things for which you've spent money. You can get this information as you review again each cancelled check and your itemized charge statements.

You don't have to write down the expenditures for the last six months. You're only going after significant items for which you chose to spend money. You can forget about listing rent or mortgage payments, fixed or other basic living expenses. And you don't have to be specific down to the penny. You can round off amounts. Leave out the really small items, too. However, put down the full cost incurred, not the amount you chose to pay that month.

What should you list? Put down luxuries, of course: travel, nonessential clothes, camera or hobby expenses, club dues, memberships, subscriptions. You need to list gifts, long-distance phone calls, furniture or other household equipment. You're going after all spending that reflects your priorities. For instance, you may have felt that new living-room furniture was essential because you've just moved into a new home. Nonetheless, it was a choice you made. You could have chosen to do without or to use thrift-shop furniture for a while. Put down all expenses above ten dollars that you weren't absolutely required to make or that you could have deferred without incurring a penalty.

Here's the worksheet for you to copy into your notebook.

SIX-MONTH ANALYSIS: STEP TWO

MONTH	SIGNIFICANT SPENDING		QUESTIONS/INSIGHTS
	AMOUNT	ITEM	

You'll notice that there's no specific amount of space assigned for each month. That's because you don't know how much there will be to list in any given month until you begin to write things down. Start with the current month and work your way back through preceding ones. When you run out of space at the bottom of the page, you can start another sheet.

Your only objective for now is to fill in amounts and items in the Significant Spending column. Remember, don't put down everything you've spent — just items of choice. You may also want to indicate the amount of down payments and to note which items were charged.

Here are some typical things you might list in any given month:

$ 40	Birthday gift
120	Clothes (charge card)
60	Motel for weekend vacation (charge card)
30	Lawn mowing expense

18	Magazine subscription
300	Chair for living room (down payment $50)
10	Party lunch at office

Of course, you will have a written record only for those items paid for by charge or by check. By all means, however, include any significant items you can recall that were paid in cash. In the future, you may find it useful to jot down important cash expenditures and keep this record with your bank statements. An alternative is to make more of such purchases by charge or by check.

In going through this exercise one more time to record my own expenditures, I found a surprise. Somewhere along the line I've become programmed to say yes to all those appeals for membership in scientific or cultural organizations. I've joined almost everything in the alphabet, starting with Art Museum Association. I'll have to put myself in a much more critical frame of mind or perhaps set an arbitrary limit beyond which I won't spend. When I add up the total cost of all those memberships I have to admit this spending won't pass the Congruence Test. I'm not putting my money where I say my priorities are.

You may discover some insights about your spending just from writing down the choices you've made over the past six months. Let's take a look at what Debra learned from the second step of her Six-Month Analysis. Here's her spending record. She pointed out that none of this includes any cash spending, only money spent by check or by charge.

MONTH	SIGNIFICANT SPENDING		QUESTIONS/INSIGHTS
Sept.	$ 41	Cosmetics (charged)	
	10	Concert	
	110	Transportation	Use van-pool regularly
	100	Gift to parents	
	261		

Aug.	45	New dishes (cups)	
	50	Books, cosmetics, nylons	
	___		
	95		
July	55	*Phone calls	High cash month because of brother and other houseguests
	67	Gifts	
	122		
June	26	Theater tickets	
	12	Concert	
	38		
May	185	Car repair (charged)	High cash month because parents were
	145	Dishes (charged)	here
	32	*Phone calls	
	25	Theater tickets	
	387		
April	95	Car repair (charged)	
	26	Theater tickets	
	58	*Phone calls	
	30	Books and records	*Long distance calls to friends are costly but definitely worthwhile
	100	Tahoe vacation	
	309		

Here are some of Debra's insights about the monthly variations in her spending and the kinds of items that showed up. "I learned from this that my high cash month was when my parents were staying here," she said. "And then there was another month when my brother and sister-in-law were here. I wanted to show them everything so that they would love San Francisco as I do and understand why I wanted to move three thousand miles away. I've also had visits from friends, but these months didn't seem to have as much cash outgo."

Debra has also found that much of her installment buying came about because of needed repairs for her car. "After I'd put a lot of miles on it driving across the country, I found myself at the mercy of unknown garage mechanics," she explained. "For instance, I paid for a tune-up and then had to pay again to have it redone somewhere else because the first place had messed it up."

She also had to cope with the replacement of a muffler and the cost of new shocks. She spent ninety-two dollars for the replacement of one windshield wiper. The wiper had been vandalized and the repair method was very costly. Finally, she was involved in an accident. This was covered by insurance, but she had to pay the first two hundred dollars.

"If something needs to be done to the car, I'm usually in trouble. I have to use my charge card," Debra said. Repairs on a car, of course, are living expenses and should be anticipated, but few of us do this. It's quite common to let such living expenses become debts.

Perhaps Debra's most valuable insights about her expenses related to her commute to work. She usually goes by van-pool, for which she pays a flat fee of fifty-six dollars per month. This is a fixed expense, whether or not she shows up to ride with the group.

"I had to look at how much it was costing me on those days when I decided to drive my car to work," she said. "Some mornings I'm just not out there in time, and any day I drive it costs me about seven dollars for the gas alone." Debra pointed out that she chooses to drive on some days when she wants her own car at noon or has planned to stay for a social event after work. She also admitted that some days she just doesn't get out of bed early enough.

"This came to a head one week recently when I slept a little longer and drove to work three days in a row," she said. "But

I don't want to let this sort of expense continue. This is one of those things that's hidden in my cash outlay, in gas costs and tolls. I think I'd rather get out of bed in time and use the money for something else."

Debra also became more alert to how much of her income had gone for interest on charge accounts. "Last spring I decided to quit charging. I've paid off three of my accounts, but I did just recently give myself a reward of more than forty dollars in cosmetics that I charged. But I do plan to continue paying off my accounts."

All in all, Debra's Six-Month Analysis shows that she's doing quite well on the Congruence Test. Her first ten-item dream list did not show all of the things she wanted, but her spending is quite congruent with what she said she wanted when she made her detailed lists by categories.

Nonetheless, she did discover some significant money leaks. She's decided to repair these leaks by keeping a lid on her commuting costs and cutting back on charge purchases. She found one expenditure she was going to make (the coffee table) that was really not her own wish but something someone else thought she ought to have. She's also found that she really does think it will be worthwhile to track her cash expenditures to understand her spending better and perhaps discover some more money leaks. Finally, she's decided to talk with others in the family about plans for providing for her parents.

How about you?

What, specifically, can you learn from your analysis? Here's the way to check for spending mistakes.

You should, like Debra, have been able to spot any spending you were about to do that fell into the Aha! category because it was programmed by your gender, your generation, your family upbringing, or one of your friends.

Here's what else to look for. Check carefully for gorilla-in-the-rain spending, perfectionism or self-esteem spending, aimless zigzagging, and instances in which you may have succumbed to advertising or merchandising pressures. As you identify mistakes, mark them in the Insights/Questions column.

Now go back for one final review of the entire thing. You may want to mark places where you think there was a conflict between logic and intuition. Study these expenditures for further clues to your approach to spending.

You may want to consider again whether any of the information from the chapter about trouble spots and transitions can offer insights that apply to your spending.

Make some preliminary decisions about how you plan to handle recurring expenses such as car repairs. You'll probably find that you need a slightly larger cash reserve if you're to keep such items off of your charge-card bills.

You may discover, as Debra did, that you'll want to study your cash flow a little more carefully. Maybe you've been succumbing to something like the fast-food expedient or some other needless but routine pattern. A listing of cash expenses will, of course, document what's happening.

Finally, do you have any major and costly gaps in communication with others in your life or unresolved personal problems? Consider that it will be less costly in the long run to start solving problems rather than persisting in spending patterns that aren't buying satisfaction but are only the by-products of other unresolved problems.

Now at last we're coming to the final and most important question of all. How will you do on the Congruence Test?

As you did your Six-Month Analysis you probably noticed some items in your spending that were not congruent with your priorities. You may already have noted these in your Questions /Insights column. Now, however, is the time to write down everything you did right.

This will be a careful, systematic assessment. Get out your notebook and review the lists itemizing your goals for Security, Caring for Others, Buyables, and Leisure that you wrote in Chapter Two. You may also want to review the Worksheet for Six-Month Planning that you filled out in Chapter Four. It's time to see if you're moving toward the goals you said were important.

Check the spending you've listed for the last six months. Where you find spending that moves you toward your goals, mark it with an important-looking circle on your Six-Month Analysis. Indulge yourself if you want. Use a bright highlight marker, or a big felt pen, or even a child's crayon. Each item you mark is a triumph! You've overcome the needs and pressures of everyday life to move a little closer to where you'd like to be. You're doing just fine on the Congruence Test.

10.

Getting Your Family
Into the Picture

W HAT HAPPENS to all of your lists and audits when you try to integrate the wishes of the whole family and get started on a spending plan? Once plans are made, it may not be harder for a family to pass the Congruence Test than it is for a single person. However, marshaling objectives and setting priorities are complicated when more than one person is involved. Keeping track of spending is likely to be a more time-consuming task, too.

Let's look at what happened with one family.

Homer and Maureen P. have a spending picture that's complicated indeed. They have just made a big change in their lives, a change that's required them to face up to some major conflicts in what they feel is important and what they should do with their money.

Homer recently inherited some money, and they've used this to make the down payment on a five-acre country place where they hope to be more self-sufficient in terms of food and energy. This past summer they sold their home in Fresno, in California's San Joaquin Valley, and moved with their two children to their new home in the foothills about an hour's drive from the city.

They are both delighted with the quiet rural surroundings, the rolling hills studded with oak trees, and the prospects for a complete change in school environment for their bright eight-year-old son, Jerry.

Homer has been absorbed in thoughts of planting a much bigger and better vegetable garden than he's ever had before. He's also talking about fruit trees, keeping hens and turkeys, and using the irrigated pasture for beef cattle.

Maureen has been enthusiastic about their new home, too, except for the prospect of keeping house in a cramped make-do situation. Actually their new home is nothing more than an oversized two-car garage with one upstairs bedroom, and an improvised kitchen, living room, and bathroom downstairs. Alongside it is the site and foundation for a large home with a view of the valley below. The previous owners, a retired couple, had started the home, but the wife became ill and died before more than temporary quarters had been built. The place had been vacant for some time.

"We couldn't have afforded to buy so much land if the former owners had managed to build that dream home of theirs," Homer told me.

Homer has kept his job. He works in a local mental health program and now commutes an hour each way to work. Maureen has also kept her position as a half-time instructor in nursing at a nearby state university. Their life was already busy and complicated, and it's even more so since they moved in August to their new home.

There are conflicts, too. Homer is passionately devoted to his farming activities but says the inner workings of the house matter very little to him. Maureen, on the other hand, yearns not only for a more convenient arrangement for housekeeping but also for beautiful things in their home.

August was a particularly difficult month for her. The weather was quite hot, and their little home has no air conditioning. She struggled to get everything unpacked and arranged in a much smaller space. She also had to keep a bored and restless toddler amused indoors because there was no safe outdoor play area for him.

With the opening of school in September, Maureen has gone back to work, and it's the busiest time of year for her as she's in charge of the program in which she's teaching. Life with the younger son is easier, however, as he loves the opportunity to play with other children that his days at the babysitter provide. Jerry's school situation brings mixed reviews, but prospects are optimistic. He's in a once-small school district in which enrollment has recently doubled. He is now awaiting assignment to a newly formed class for gifted children.

I think that Homer and Maureen's experience this summer might have posed serious difficulty in a less stable and affectionate marriage, but they are very fond of each other and determined to reap the benefits of their new lifestyle. "This may sound crazy to some people," Maureen told me, "but I'd do it all over again."

Nonetheless, some important issues remain unresolved. Homer is squeezed for time and money to establish the farming operation, and Maureen wants more amenities in their home. Each purchase they make, one way or the other, seems almost a negation of the other's wishes.

Homer and Maureen were both interested in the ideas I'd been explaining to them, but were reluctant to try my planning lists and worksheets because their time is so precious. They also worried that they weren't typical enough or wouldn't be a good example because their lives had just changed so much.

They reported afterward that this project couldn't have come at a better time for them, and it has helped them make some important decisions and changes. They did say, however, that inventorying their expenses took longer than I had indicated. I'm not surprised, considering the complexity of their situation.

They started right at the beginning with the ideas in the early chapters of this book. They made out their first dream lists, and wrote separate lists of objectives in accordance with the four categories I've established: Security, Caring for Others, Buyables, and Leisure. They worked briefly to learn the procedure for the Monthly Audit and then reviewed the Worksheet for Six-Month Planning, including the roots review and the search for possible substitutions.

After this, they did the two-stage Six-Month Analysis.

Step One, with information about the amounts of money they had been spending, surprised them. They had expected their monthly expenses to go down after they sold their home in

Fresno and no longer had to meet two mortgage payments. This was not the case, however, because other spending was increasing. Their monthly cash outlay stayed about the same, averaging some $470 each month. Their not-cash spending was about $2,100 per month.

Their installment debt is going up, from just under $800 at the start of the six months to about $1050. They've stepped up their monthly payments, however, from less than $50 to about $400.

Maureen and Homer, by my guess, are now spending about $500 per month more than their take-home pay.

"I knew we were spending more than we earn," Homer said, "but I was resisting getting it all down in black and white. We'd planned to overspend for a while. We'll use the extra money as we had planned until it's gone, but we'd really like to make the best possible use of it."

If they fail eventually to make a match between their income and their living expenses they will, of course, be practicing brinksmanship. I doubt, however, that they will fall into this trap. Their basic objective as they go through this unique time in their lives, as Homer has said, is to achieve the best possible alignment between their most important priorities and their actual use of money — in short, to pass the Congruence Test.

Step Two of their Six-Month Analysis, in which they listed the significant items for which they'd spent money, showed some spending that didn't match their objectives. You may find it useful to see what they put down on Step Two of that analysis.

MONTH	SIGNIFICANT SPENDING	
Sept.	$ 47	MGM Grand—show
	110	Motel and meals
	74	Seeds
	185	Doors, hinges, paint
	10	Book
	111	Sprinklers, field fencing

	9	Meals out
	45	Seeder
	$591	
Aug.	$ 9	Play tickets
	21	Hairdresser
	36	Meals out
	21	Garbage can
	$ 87	
July	$ 51	Meals out
	65	Housecleaning
	91	Tools and building supplies
	11	Magazine subscription
	80	Rafting trip
	27	Soil amendment
	23	Grass catcher
	36	Trees
	$384	
June	$ 29	Magazine subscriptions
	79	Hardware, screws, etc.
	89	Meals out
	24	Hairdresser
	93	Hammock
	$314	
May	$ 19	Photo processing
	18	Photo albums
	74	Housecleaning
	61	Lawn care and equipment
	51	Meals out
	8	Musical tickets
	4	Faucet top
	32	Equipment rental
	5	Ice cream
	$272	
April	$ 45	Lawn mower
	70	Housecleaning
	10	Photo processing

8	Ice cream
65	Trees
19	Chicken wire and hardware
50	Cabinets
38	Lawn mower repair
$305	

This part of Homer and Maureen's Six-Month Analysis shows that their spending didn't always match their objectives. Maureen felt they had been spending too much for recreation away from home. On their Labor Day weekend at Lake Tahoe they spent more than $150 for lodging, meals, and admission to a show. "This bothers me," Maureen said, "because we have different recreational needs. I'd rather stay home and put the house in order." Homer, on the other hand, says, "When I take time off from work I really want to get away."

They admitted another mistake made on their Labor Day weekend. "That was just nuts," Homer said, "that bike we bought. When we rented bikes we learned the rental place had an expensive bike in good shape to sell because this was the end of the season. It was just a fine bike — $65 for something worth $300. Each of us has a bike, but we bought it anyhow." Keeping that bike might be a gorilla-in-the-rain mistake. Homer and Maureen could probably recoup at least $100 by selling it.

This is an item that didn't show up on their Six-Month Analysis because they paid cash for it. As with any spending record, theirs is incomplete. In Homer and Maureen's case, much of his spending is done in cash, while she has a habit of paying for nearly everything by check or by charge. They will be able to get a more accurate picture of their spending in the future if Homer decides to keep a record of his cash outlays or pay for more items by check or by charge.

What else did they learn from this part of their Six-Month Analysis? They found that since they've moved they're spending much more for tools and garden supplies. Their average spending in this category was less than $150 per month for the first five months, but then shot up to over $400 for the last month.

What changes might they make?

They both want to cut down on meals out, which have been averaging over $50 per month. They've decided to cut down on magazine subscriptions, too, and Maureen says she will cut down on going to the hairdresser. She also suggested cutting down on housecleaning expenses, but Homer eventually decided to put this back into their spending plan.

It's obvious that small economies will only be a part of the answer. Homer and Maureen will need to continue keeping careful track of their spending so they can get a better idea of how much is going for living expenses in their new home and how much is being spent for one-time "establishing" costs. If they borrow money or use up all of their surplus to improve their present home, this will become especially crucial.

The next step for Homer and Maureen was to follow the procedure you will follow next. They went back to the lists of what they wanted in terms of Security, Caring for Others, Buyables, and Leisure, and added to these lists an indicator by each item to show whose needs the objectives were intended to serve.

Take out the lists that you wrote by categories, and use this worksheet to rewrite them.

REVISED LIST OF OBJECTIVES (Name _____)

SOURCE			CATEGORY	ITEM
Own	Joint	Part		

Make a separate worksheet for each member of the family and be sure to keep all the worksheets in your notebook. Take as much space as you need and add additional pages until you're done. Start with Security.

As you rewrite your lists, indicate whether an item is your very own, is something both you and your partner want, or is included only because it is something you feel is important to your partner. Yes, I know that I asked you to make out your lists entirely on your own. But if you're like many others, it's more than likely you've put down some things for your partner. Separate ideas by what you believe to be their sources. You'll see that there are valuable insights to be gained — and money to be conserved — by being clear about who wants what and why.

Here's what Homer and Maureen put on their lists.

REVISED LIST OF OBJECTIVES: Homer

SOURCE			CATEGORY	ITEM
Own	Joint	Part		
			Security	
		x		New house
x				Energy self-sufficiency
x				Food self-sufficiency
x				Write on farm and garden topics

X				Retirement farm in Costa Rica
X				Ranch for people who want to be healthy
X				Appropriate schooling for Jerry
X				Train for counseling certificate in order to work at home

Caring for Others

X				Have time for children
X				Bring Maureen's parents to California to live

Buyables

X				One year of travel
X				Sail around the world
X				Sports car
X				Rolls Royce
X				Solar home
X				Home by the sea
X				Mountain home
X				Collect beautiful art objects
X				Fencing for garden
X				Chicken coop

Own	Joint	Part		
x				Turkey pen
x				Fruit trees
			Leisure	
x				Time to shop for collectibles
x				Karate classes with Jerry
x				Ski trip

REVISED LIST OF OBJECTIVES: Maureen

SOURCE			CATEGORY	ITEM
Own	Joint	Part		
			Security	
	x			Energy self-sufficiency
	x			Invest for retirement
x				Continue at present job
x				Additional professional training:
				1. As Pediatric Nurse Practioner
				2. Ph.D.
			Caring for Others	
x				Bring parents to California for vacation
x				Help sister get established

Own	Joint	Part	Category	Item
			Buyables	
x				New or remodeled house
	x			Oak chairs to match dining table
	x			Sofa bed
	x			Painting by local artist
			Leisure	
x				Housecleaning help
x				Child-care services

REVISED LIST OF OBJECTIVES: Jerry

Source Own	Joint	Part	Category	Item
			Buyables	
x				A horse
			Leisure	
x				Karate classes

As you look over Homer and Maureen's lists, you will see some differences in their perceptions of what they want and in their approach to their objectives. It's obvious they haven't checked with each other on the objectives they listed as Joint or Partner's. This is true of most couples. It's also obvious they have another problem that nearly always emerges when two people try to set priorities: equity.

At this stage in the development of their plans, Homer has declared a wide-ranging and imaginative set of objectives for himself, while Maureen is centered on family and career and most particularly on their housing situation. We talked about this. "I really can't expand my thinking much right now," she told me, "because I'm so focused on doing something about our house."

Maureen was delighted that Homer had written down having

a better home as her objective. Actually, his thinking seemed to be evolving even while they were talking about their lists. "All along," he said, "I'd been thinking that I didn't care what was indoors at our place and that I just wanted to keep the mortgage as small as possible. But I guess I can't even really say that a nicer home is just Maureen's objective. I'm beginning to think of it as an investment."

He also agreed that the lack of privacy in their present home bothered him as much as it bothered Maureen, and he wanted to do something about it. Homer had been considering installing a partition in the upstairs bedroom. "It's become clear," he reported, "that when we've talked about remodeling, we haven't been talking about the same thing. Maureen wants much more than I do."

She agreed. "When I let myself dream about what I want in a house," she said, "I find most of my images relate to the kitchen. I want a beautiful vinyl floor in a warm color. I want an island for the stove, and I want a second sink with a pass-through window to the outside for washing vegetables from the garden."

Both agreed on the desirability of a solar home. Homer had listed this (along with a mountain home and a seashore home) on his list of Buyables. He emphasized the practical aspects of a solar home. "But I like the aesthetics," Maureen said, "with a whole high wall of glass. I like the idea, too, of plants hanging down. For the rest of the house I'm more interested in good design than in expensive decorating."

In any family, objectives can differ, priorities can differ, and the fair allotment of the spendable money can be a knotty problem. I've seen marriages in which it seems as if the man brings home all the money and never has a voice in how it's spent. I've seen others in which the man's interests seem to predominate and the woman's are limited to tending the family and equipping the home.

In some cases appearances can be deceiving. The selection of priorities may be more or less underground, but the actual spending of money may work out with some equity. Loving partners *do* look after each other's interests. However, this is an indirect system for achieving equity, and it's less likely to be efficient than an open and direct system. Often people are not accurate in their perceptions of what their partners want.

In other cases there may be a genuine imbalance. Some people can be thoughtless when it comes to using the family resources, and others can be unduly reticent when it comes to speaking up for their own needs. The writing down of goals and the making of plans to achieve these goals, however, carries with it the idea that each person will get a fair shake. Once both partners have agreed to start getting things in writing, those individuals whose objectives aren't fairly represented usually find they have a framework for constructive discussion of the situation. We'll see, as we watch Homer and Maureen develop their plans, that their selection of spending priorities moves toward a balance.

Also, Homer told me that getting all of his plans in writing had been very useful to him. "I tend to get things jammed up in my mind," he said, "and to think about things over and over again and not do anything. I hate that. Now that I've planned things out, I realize I'll need the same kind of fence for turkey and chicken coops as I do for the garden. I'll save both time and money if I consolidate and buy everything at once."

There's one final point for you to consider about your own separate lists. Be wary of a general goal for which you do not have in mind any specific steps for achieving it — or any lesser version that might make you happy. It may be that such a general goal is unrealistic. I think this was the case with Homer when he put down that he wanted a sports car and a Rolls Royce. His taste in vehicles (as well as in other things) usually runs to practicality and economy. Why should he list cars in the luxury class? The answer may be "just because." Most of us follow conventional ideas and think we want certain items. We usually discard at least some of them, however, when we get down to planning the details of our spending.

When you've finished reviewing your separate lists you're ready for the next important step: your Merged List of Objectives. The speed with which your family's combined list can be put together should please you. You may discover areas in which you and others in your family are surprisingly in agreement on what you want.

Will there be problems? Not really, at this stage. Your goal will be to list everything everybody wants. If everything is to go on the list, there won't be any disagreements about what must be left out. Be ready, however, to toss out a few goals you discover aren't really important to you.

You won't have room on your Merged List to detail all of the specifics of your objectives. It's important that you have thought through these details, but now select a key phrase that describes each objective in a few words.

Here's a sample of the form for you to use and keep in your notebook.

MERGED LIST OF OBJECTIVES

CATEGORY	SHARED OBJECTIVES	INDIVIDUAL OBJECTIVES

Start a separate sheet for each of the categories. You'll not likely run out of space on one sheet for either Security or Caring for Others, but I expect Buyables and Leisure may require several pages. Leave plenty of extra room. You'll be keeping these lists for quite a while, adding items as they come up and perhaps crossing off things you've accomplished or about which you've changed your mind. Also, there may be times when a rather general goal is later subdivided into more specific elements to be achieved in sequence.

Homer and Maureen told me that it took them less than an hour to compile their Merged List of Objectives. They reported they found out that they had more goals in common than they had realized. "We sparked each other as we made out our lists of shared objectives," Maureen told me. "For instance, we identified as an important objective having more time together away from all our responsibilities, even though we want to keep the costs down."

They discarded some objectives, too. "We threw out silly things like the Rolls Royce," Homer said. "I don't know yet what we're going to leave out that's really important to either of us. We didn't make any forced choices. We just put some things further into the future."

Here's what their Merged List of Objectives looked like.

MERGED LIST OF OBJECTIVES

Category	Shared Objectives	Individual Objectives	
Security	Energy self-sufficiency Invest for retirement	His:	Food self-sufficiency Farm, Costa Rica Write Ranch (health) School for son Counseling certificate

		Hers:	Continue working
			PNP training
			Doctorate
Caring for Others	Parents to California	His:	Time for kids
		Hers:	Parents' vacation
			Help sister
Buyables	Solar home (new or remodeled)	His:	Sail around world
			Sports car
	One year travel		Sea home
			Mountain home
	Buy painting		Chicken coop
	Fence for garden		Turkey pen
			Pig
	Cows	Hers:	Oak dining chairs
			Sofa
		Son:	Horse
Leisure	Housecleaning	His:	Karate class (with son)
	Time out together		Ski trip
		Hers:	Child care

As I talked with Homer and Maureen about the priorities they'd identified on their merged list, we could see some compromises they'd probably be making when it came time to work from this list and develop a new spending plan. Let's look first at some of the insights they gained with this Merged List of Objectives.

Their continuing indecision about whether or not to have a new house is, of course, taking most of their attention. They have considered buying another piece of property in the same neighborhood. "It has an absolutely spectacular view," Maureen told me, "but the house on the property is an undistinguished version of a tract home." Homer has reservations about this other place, too. "I'd have to sacrifice all the improvements I've already made in the yard, and the other place doesn't have an irrigated pasture," he said.

Also important to Homer is the start that's already been made on the property they now own, the concrete foundation for a beautiful large home. "We've picnicked out there a few times on warm evenings, and the view is nice enough," he said. "More important, the existing foundation and water and electric connections are worth at least seven thousand dollars."

Homer and Maureen have decided to invite her cousin, who is an architect, to visit them in a few weeks when he comes to California on a consulting assignment. "We'll send him plans of this place and lists of our ideas," they told me, "and we think we'll soon have a lot more information on which to base a decision. Maybe we can come up with a construction plan that can be accomplished in stages."

In the meantime, they've been able to reach some other conclusions. A surprise for both of them was how much they wanted some paintings by the artist that Maureen had included on her list. Homer, who had put "Collect beautiful art objects" on his original list, told me they still recalled in great detail the artist's work. "I think we'd be smart to buy those two paintings we saw that we especially liked," he said, "or accept as an alternative some other paintings by her."

Homer also commented on the ways his perceptions had changed as they'd made their lists. "For years," he said, "I've thought I wanted those oak chairs, too. "Well, I really don't care whether we ever have them or not."

Also, when they made their Merged List he added animals as well as the gardening, poultry, and fruit trees. Obviously she didn't share his enthusiasm. When he wrote "Pig" she reached over and wrote "Poo!" She added an astute observation. "Everybody in our neighborhood is now trying to get started raising animals," she pointed out. "For the short term, I think we may be able to buy some good bargains on the hoof when our neighbors discover they've raised more than they can use."

Homer surprised Maureen when he insisted on putting back into the list some housecleaning help, which she had dropped as a measure to conserve money. Looking at her fondly he said, "This I can see as my own personal objective. It's worth it to me. When you're busy and the house is a mess, you're crabby." This seems to be another instance in which an objective Homer had considered to be Maureen's turned out to be something he, too, wants them to have.

There was a lot of give and take, and there were also some changes in the items they listed as objectives. A spirit of compromise was evident. They are not yet to the stage of making immediate spending plans, but they bantered in a friendly style about whether she would settle for getting a secondhand sofa if he would agree to defer purchase of the turkey pen.

What about you?

Your own situation is undoubtedly quite different. Nonetheless, Homer and Maureen's experience, and the experiences of others, offers a check list for you to consider as you give your Merged List of Objectives one final review.

Have you left anything out of your lists? You've worked your way through a lengthy process, starting with that first dream list, progressing to a list by categories and a six-month spending plan. You've rewritten your separate lists and made a combined list. Make sure you haven't simply forgotten something. Also, you shouldn't be too ready to toss out wilder ideas or longer-term objectives unless you're absolutely certain you no longer want them.

Have you shorted any person? Maureen, whose style is different from Homer's, kept her list to a minimum because she focuses on immediate priorities. Family members who focus on short-term goals or tend to be reticent may need some encouragement to list everything they want.

Did you find that your plans for helping someone in the family need to be clarified? (Debra, and also Maureen and Homer, discovered they not only needed to talk with others in the family but also with those parents they planned to help.)

Did you find you were planning to do something for someone else when it wasn't particularly important to that other person?

Did you find you were counting on someone else to state a goal you've had in mind all along, but he or she didn't?

Did you discover, as Homer did in regard to having an improved home, that a goal you've been thinking was someone else's was actually important to you?

Can you (at least in your mind) subdivide rather general goals into specific steps to achieve them? If not, better put a question mark by that goal.

Now you're ready for the final procedure. It's time to set short-term priorities and make actual spending plans in keeping with the amount of money you have available. This will be the ultimate step in the series of audits and worksheets I've asked you to do.

11.

Putting It All
into Motion

YOU ARE READY at last for the plan that will be the
culmination of all you've done so far. This final step will set
you up on a permanent system of priority-setting and month-
by-month planning and auditing of your expenditures.

This will be a two-stage procedure. The first stage will be to
put all your goals together in a dollars-and-cents projection for
achieving them. The second stage will be to develop, every
month, plans that take into account the money you have available. Provisions will be made for unplanned extras, and you will
be given ways to measure your progress and fine-tune next
month's spending.

The first stage, your Spending Projection, will resemble the
Worksheet for Six-Month Planning you made back in Chapter
Four, but there'll be some important differences. You've
learned a great deal since then — how to think through your
spending decisions and how to avoid money traps and unsatisfy-
ing spending. You've learned how some other people have been
examining their problems, dreams, and spending plans. Most
important, you've learned how to apply the Congruence Test
to your spending.

This is the time for you to gather together all of the materials
you've worked on so far. Starting with the first part of this book,
here are the worksheets I've asked you to do.

Chapter Two: Your first dream list and your first list by those
four categories.

Chapter Four: Your Monthly Audit and Worksheet for Six-Month Planning.

Chapter Nine: Your Six-Month Analysis, Step One for amounts and Step Two for significant items.

Chapter Ten: Your Revised List of Objectives, listing sources of those objectives, and your Merged List of Objectives. You did not do these if you are living alone.

If you are working as a family, you will start with your Merged List of Objectives. If you have only yourself to plan for and have not reviewed your Categorized Lists since you first wrote them (that was back in Chapter Two), you should review them now. Your perceptions may have changed or your objectives become more clearly defined.

Now, as you prepare your Spending Projection, your time frame will be less rigid than it was on your Worksheet for Six-Month Planning. Record in detail what you want to do soonest and include your best estimate of the price tag for each objective. Allow yourself a range of a year or more, with your plans becoming less specific as you go further into the future.

You're going to transfer several items selected from your Categorized List of Objectives or your Merged List of Objectives to the Spending Projection worksheet on the next page.

You may find it helpful first to sort out your thinking by taking a separate piece of paper and going through your lists. Note briefly the items that have absolutely top priority for you. Look especially for major items for which you will need to set aside money regularly.

Once you've noted your top priorities — the things that are most important and that seem most appropriate for you to begin to accomplish within the coming year or so — you should write down a few smaller objectives. Consider some small-but-pleasant items that will bring nice benefits in enjoyment and for which the cost can be fitted in rather easily. You may want to note a few objectives that will require specific timing, for instance taking advantage of seasonal sales and making yard or garden improvements while the weather is right.

You are probably working, at least in part, from your original Worksheet for Six-Month Planning. This plan had spaces for a

SPENDING PROJECTION

ESTIMATED COST	ITEM	TIMING

review of your spending roots and also for possible substitutions. You should still be aware of these, but you should no longer need such "training wheels." Nonetheless, you should continue to use these principles for screening and refining your objectives.

Your first step in transferring items from your separate trial list to your Spending Projection is to take care of Security items. Determine what is essential and get these things down first. It's important to include monthly allocations for goals such as reducing an installment debt load or beginning to build a contingency or investment fund. Even if you can allocate only a few dollars, allocate something.

Once you've taken care of Security, you can move on to Caring for Others, Buyables, and Leisure. Be realistic but not overly cautious. Lean a little in the direction of planning more than you might be able to do. This is all right, as long as you plan to do the most important items first and schedule others as they can be achieved. If you are highly motivated about achieving some of your objectives, you may be pleasantly surprised at how far you can cut back on other spending that isn't so important to you.

You may be interested in seeing how the Spending Projection worked out for those people I've talked about in previous chapters. Debra's projection was tightly organized and focused closely on the immediate future. Here's what she put down.

COST	ITEM	TIMING
$50/mo.	Financial help for parents	Now (increase when some bills are paid)
$25/mo.	Tickets for theater, etc.	Now (this is limit until bills are paid)
$400	Trip to Boston	Two months
$100	Trip to Oregon	Three months
$150	Bookcase	Four months (from expected promotion & raise)
$150	Painting or prints	Six months (income tax refund)
$50–$75	Coral ring	When I see one I love
$7600	New car	One year (reward for sticking to plan)

When I compared Debra's Spending Projection with her Six-Month Analysis, I saw that she had done some realistic thinking. For example, she allocated twenty-five dollars per month for theater and concert tickets. That ties in rather closely with what's she's been spending. Now that she's set a regular amount for herself, however, I expect she'll feel more relaxed about making ticket-purchase decisions. She won't have to feel guilty about spending what she spends, and she's also given herself flexibility because she can save and borrow from her ticket budget. She's also achieved a good balance between what she plans to spend to furnish her apartment and her other objectives. Finally, she's set up rewards for herself for sticking to her plan.

The Spending Projection that Homer and Maureen made is, of course, much more wide-ranging and also much more tentative. They prefaced their list with a notation that they would make a decision about their home within a year. They will spend at the very least $15,000 for remodeling and at most $75,000 for new construction.

We're just not going to know the outcome of some major decisions they have yet to make. Nonetheless, here's how their Spending Projection has helped them organize their thinking so far.

COST	ITEM	TIMING
$15–75,000	Housing	Within one year
$1750	Food self-sufficiency (chicken coop, turkey pen, fruit trees, garden fence, cow, pig)	Over next two years, but starting now with items in sequence
$40/mo.	Housecleaning twice monthly	Now
$500	Sofa	Two weeks
$40/mo.	Karate classes (Homer and Jerry)	Two months

$50	Rent house trailer for parent's visit	Two months
$100	Ski trip	Three months
$50	Help sister get established (phone calls, extra food)	Three months
?	Private school for Jerry	Investigate now; start in six months if needed
?	Oak chairs	One year
$15,000	Counseling certificate for Homer (main cost is salary loss)	Begin in two years

For Homer and Maureen a lot of decisions are still up in the air, the first and most far-reaching being what they will do about their living quarters. Maureen has started to talk, too, about going back to work full time. In addition to the extra salary this will bring directly, she also points out that as long as she stays on part-time status she will not be in line to progress to the higher salary that would be hers with full-time tenure. The projection they have made, however, sets forth their priorities by determining the sequence in which purchases will be made. This plan also resolves to some degree how much Homer will be spending for the food-growing improvements he so fiercely wants. He's agreed to stay within a specific budget.

Once you've drafted your Spending Projection, you'll be ready to try your first combined Monthly Plan and Audit. This is the second part of your two-stage procedure.

Before you start, however, you'll need some information about how much money you're going to have available after you've taken care of routine and necessary expenses. You've already done the fact-finding that will enable you to make some fairly exact estimates. You did this with your Six-Month Analysis in Chapter Nine. All you have to do now is pull out this information.

This is the time to go back to those worksheets you've kept in your notebook. You're going to estimate how much you'll be spending each month in cash and also how much you'll need for routine bills.

Here's how this might work out. As an example, I'll use a single young man with take-home pay of some $1400 per month. This is what Step One of his Six-Month Analysis showed.

MONTH	CASH TOTAL	NOT-CASH TOTAL
One	$ 500	$ 890
Two	380	960
Three	420	990
Four	460	1090
Five	410	896
Six	395	1005
	2565	5831

The monthly average of his Cash spending is, of course, the sum of the monthly Cash totals divided by six. That comes to an average Cash outlay each month of $427.50.

Determining the cost of routine and necessary Not-Cash spending takes a little more arithmetic. It also requires information from Step Two of the Six-Month Analysis. Here's the needed information.

MONTH	SIGNIFICANT SPENDING TOTAL
One	$ 545
Two	95

Three	122
Four	253
Five	387
Six	289
	1691

Now we're ready for the arithmetic. From Step One we have a six-month total of all Not-Cash spending of $5831. We subtract the six-month total of Significant Spending, which is $1691. This remainder tells us how much was routine and necessary spending. It's $4140, or $690 each month.

Here's a summary of the procedure for you to use.

To determine Cash spending:
1. Use Step One to learn how much was spent in cash for the six months.
2. Divide by six.

To determine routine expenses not paid in cash:
1. Use Step One to learn how much was spent altogether in the Not-Cash category.
2. Use Step Two to learn how much went for Significant Spending.
3. Subtract the six-month sum of Significant Spending from the six-month sum of Not-Cash spending.
4. Divide by six.

You now have a basis for calculating how much you should set aside each month for cash and for routine expenses. You'll be adding a little to this to allow for inflation.

There's one more step you may want to take before you do your Monthly Plan and Audit. This relates to installment debt. Your installment payments are included in your routine Not-Cash spending record. If you want to increase the rate at which you'll be paying off these debts, determine a target amount to put in your plans.

Now you're ready for this worksheet to add to your notebook.

MONTHLY PLAN AND AUDIT

CATEGORY	ESTIMATE	ACTUAL AMOUNT
INCOME		
Salary		
Other Sources		
Total		
ROUTINE SPENDING		
Cash		
Not Cash		
Extra installment payment		
Total		
AVAILABLE FOR SIGNIFICANT SPENDING		
PLANNED SIGNIFICANT SPENDING		

  _____

  _____

  _____

  _____

  _____

UNPLANNED SIGNIFICANT SPENDING

  _____

  _____

_____

_____

TOTAL SIGNIFICANT
SPENDING

_____

BOTTOM LINE SUMMARY: Total Income for Month   _____
                       Total Spent During Month   _____
                       Installment Debt Balance   _____

_____

Let's see how the Monthly Plan and Audit worked out for the
young man we were talking about. The first thing to enter is his
income. The amount is $1402. Then we put in the information
from his Six-Month Analysis. Average Cash spending was just
under $430, but we'll allow a little extra for inflation and enter
$460. For his Not-Cash spending we'll allow some for inflation,
too. He averaged $690, but we'll enter $720.

I haven't yet given you information about his installment
debt. It's relatively small, but has been creeping up and now
stands at $160. We'll put in a target amount of $15 extra to help
get it back down again.

Now we subtract the total estimated spending from monthly
income. This leaves an estimated $207 available for Significant
Spending.

Now items can be selected from his Spending Projection and
listed under Planned Significant Spending. He wants a new
hiking jacket, money to buy gas for a trip home, camera repair
and film, and swimming lessons. This came to a little over $200,
by his estimate. I don't think that leaves him much room for
unplanned spending, but he expects to trim expenses for food
and other things for which he pays cash.

Here's how the worksheet looked when the planning part
had been finished at the start of the month.

MONTHLY PLAN AND AUDIT

CATEGORY	ESTIMATE	ACTUAL AMOUNT
INCOME		
Salary	$1402	
Other sources	—	
Total	1402	
ROUTINE SPENDING		
Cash	460	
Not Cash	720	
Extra installment payment	15	
Total	1195	
AVAILABLE FOR SIGNIFICANT SPENDING	207	
PLANNED SIGNIFICANT SPENDING		
Hiking jacket	60	
Trip home for birthday (gas)	35	
Camera repair and film	80	
Swim lessons	30	
UNPLANNED SIGNIFICANT SPENDING		
_____		
_____		

TOTAL SIGNIFICANT
SPENDING

BOTTOM LINE SUMMARY: Total Income for Month _____
                      Total Spent During Month _____
                      Installment Debt Balance _____

This is as much as he'll be able to complete at the start of the month. The same is true for you. Here's a summary of what you should have done so far.

1. Entered estimated income from salary and other sources.
2. Adjusted Cash and routine Not-Cash spending for inflation and entered these.
3. Entered an extra amount for installment payments, if you're planning to do this.
4. Added up the total income you expect, subtracted from this the total routine spending you anticipate, and entered this as the amount available for Significant Spending.
5. Entered selected items from your Spending Projection along with the cost estimates for them.

Take a close look to see if you're being too ambitious about what you plan for Significant Spending. I recommend either that you plan for only about two thirds of the amount available or that you plan to defer some of the spending until you see how things are coming along.

You may find that you prefer to work first in pencil as you enter items from your Spending Projection. This way you can do a little arithmetic on the side and rework your choices if you decide you want to. You can fine-tune during the month in another way by planning to keep your cash outlay down and then going ahead with a purchase nearer the end of the month if you've been successful. Also, you can take a closer look at routine expenses you're anticipating. You may have a little extra this month if you're not expecting insurance bills or any other large payments; just remember to be anticipating these bills when they do come in. Once you've worked out a trial-and-error plan in pencil, enter your final spending plan and the estimates for each item.

You're now ready to go ahead and live your month and see how it all works out. You'll finish the worksheet at month's end. Here's how things worked out for that man in our example.

MONTHLY PLAN AND AUDIT

CATEGORY	ESTIMATE	ACTUAL AMOUNT
INCOME		
Salary	$1402	$1402
Other sources (cash for birthday)	—	24
Total	1402	1426
ROUTINE SPENDING		
Cash	460	445
Not Cash	720	740
Extra installment payment	15	10
Total	1195	1195
AVAILABLE FOR SIGNIFICANT SPENDING	207	231
PLANNED SIGNIFICANT SPENDING		
Hiking jacket	60	53

Trip home for birthday (gas)	35	32
Camera repair and film	80	92
Swim lessons	30	—
UNPLANNED SIGNIFICANT SPENDING		
Dinner out		27
Car battery		55
TOTAL SIGNIFICANT SPENDING	205	259

BOTTOM LINE SUMMARY: Total income for Month $1426
Total Spent During Month   1454
Installment Debt Balance   140

Let's take a look at what happened. His actual income increased by a small amount, $24 as a birthday gift. Cash spending was down by $15, but his Not-Cash spending was up to $740 (his telephone bill was larger than he'd been expecting). There was an unanticipated expense — a new car battery. At this point he decided to scale down his extra installment debt payment by $5. He also decided to postpone starting his swim lessons. This turned out to be a wise decision, because the birthday trip home produced an unexpected expense for a dinner out.

When we get to the Bottom Line Summary, we can see that he's getting his installment debt down. He'd already been paying $10 per month, he added the $10 extra installment payment, and he didn't make any new charge-card purchases. The month's spending, however, outstripped income by $28. This small deficit he can cover by the reserve in his checking account, but he's currently feeling rather cautious about next month.

At first glance it may seem that omitting that special dinner out would have neatly balanced this man's income and outgo problem. To my thinking, however, the basic problem was allotting too large a proportion of the money available for significant spending.

All of us, however, have to learn just how many unanticipated events we can anticipate in our lives. The proportions that work well for one person's planning might not for another's. As you gain experience with your own Monthly Plan and Audit, you'll likely discover about how much to allot to the various categories.

How should you proceed when you're finishing your Monthly Plan and Audit after you've lived your month? You probably won't want to wait until your bank statement comes in. You don't have to, because you can get the information you need from your check stubs and the receipts from charge purchases.

Here's how to do this, using the Monthly Audit procedure. You can get your total for Cash spending by adding up the checks you wrote for cash or at the grocery store. Include any part of your paycheck you withdrew in cash if you took it to the bank to deposit in person. Subtract your Cash spending from your monthly income. This will give you the total amount for routine Not-Cash expenses and for Significant Spending. Subtract what you spent for those significant items, and you'll have the amount for your routine Not-Cash spending. I expect you've been filling in actual amounts of your significant-item spending as the month went along. If you didn't, however, you have this information in your check stubs and charge receipts.

Once you've entered your actual income and the various categories of expenses, you'll be ready to fill in the Bottom Line Summary. You have the information for actual income and expenses, and you can refer to your charge-card statements to calculate the amount of your current installment debt.

You have now completed your Monthly Plan and Audit.

If your income was more than your outgo, take a moment to savor this accomplishment. You're moving ahead toward all of the things most important to you. I hope, too, that you enter some kind of highly visible mark for each item of spending that increases your score on the Congruence Test.

You should also devise an indicator to mark spending mistakes, perhaps a note on the bottom of your Monthly Plan and Audit. You can't avoid mistakes altogether, but you'll want to keep a record of them to provide yourself with useful insights for the future.

The information you glean from assessing the progress you've made in the past month should be helpful to you in starting the next month's plan. Work again from your Spending Projection. Have you made enough savings to accelerate your schedule for anything? Does any of your unplanned spending point out a new direction that should now be included on your Spending Projection?

Remember to keep your Spending Projection flexible. It will probably change as the months go by. Write all over it as much as you want, especially to remind yourself of your successes. If it gets too messy or there are too many changes, you can write a new list. (It should be useful, however, to keep your old lists in your notebook. You may want to review them at some time in the future.)

You may want to fiddle with the format of the Spending Projection or the Monthly Plan and Audit to make them more suitable for your particular needs. I hope you do. You may also want to look ahead to a specific time for adding up your accomplishments and making a new plan — perhaps at New Year's, when you do your income taxes, or at the start of the next fiscal year. Whatever adjustments you make you can begin to reap the rewards of the time you've spent on analysis and planning. You have become a successful spender. Enjoy!

Epilogue

Epilogue

Whatever might happen to Charlie Spender, Susan Wavering, and Norm and Shirley Proper?

These people are real enough, although I invented them. Their personalities, their styles of coping with life and spending money, and their particular situations were derived from a composite of people I've known. I shared what I had written about them with Dr. Herbert R. Harris, a clinical psychologist with more than thirty years of experience in marriage and family counseling. "Your people *are* real," he told me. "I've seen Charlie and Susan and the Propers, or people very much like them, over and over again in my office."

We talked over the kinds of money situations he most often encounters among those people who come to him for help. One typical case, he said, is the man who spends money elsewhere when it is needed at home. "This is often the man who stops at a bar after work," Dr. Harris said. "He will insist, perhaps, that spending time there is required for dealing with the customers in his business — which, of course, it seldom is." What is the most frequent situation among women who practice unproductive spending? It's that much-talked-about charge-card spending spree, according to Dr. Harris. Such situations, he said, are less frequent than misspending by men.

"These spending sprees can occur when a woman feels depressed and rejected," he explained. "But when she buys new drapes that aren't really needed or can't be afforded right then, it's only a temporary shot in the arm. She's gotten an ego boost, but soon she must go out and get another."

Dr. Harris agrees with my perspectives on Susan Wavering, Charlie Spender, and the Propers. Susan was avoiding responsibility for her own life and losing herself in a maze of zigs and zags. Charlie was giving in to those impulses to spend to shore up his ego and he was wasting money his family needed. Norm and Shirley were involved in endless dutiful spending, ignoring their own wishes and dreams, and possibly discouraging independence in their children.

I asked Dr. Harris what he thought might be the outcomes of their lives. He thinks people like Susan and Charlie face major difficulties.

"I might see a Susan in my office occasionally. Under pressure from her parents, or at the suggestion of a friend, she might decide to try 'seeing a shrink,'" he said. "However, I doubt if she would come back after the first visit or two."

Dr. Harris said he would be more optimistic about correcting this pattern if he had the opportunity to work with such an individual (male or female) in a family setting at an earlier age. "However, at this point if she did not wish to face the reality of her behavior, there is little reason to assume that her lifestyle would change," he said.

"If a person like Susan decides that change is necessary, she will have to do much of her learning on her own — face a couple of shocks, handle various situations, and feel disgusted enough with her life to actively accomplish change. Otherwise she could be repeating her same behavior at age 29, with or without marriage, children, or additional complications. Age in itself is no assurance of maturity."

He added that a person like Susan may benefit from finding herself among a circle of friends who are becoming more mature. "She may enroll in a course or two and find people who make an impression on her."

Can — or should — her parents help?

"It may be possible that her parents can improve their relationship with her without overtones of lecturing or directing," he said. "It's hard to say 'don't help' or 'cut her off.' Parents must weigh the consequences of withdrawing from the situation."

He offered one final word of encouragement. "Don't write off the Susans of this world. There are a significant number who do manage to grow up and become productive, happy adults," he said.

What did Dr. Harris have to say about Charlie?

"In a situation like Charlie Spender's, it's his wife who may have to initiate some action," he reported. "I think anyone in her situation should be madder than all get out."

Someone who lets herself get into the circumstances that Mrs. Charlie Spender faces is likely not to be a person to easily take assertive action. When the bills come in and she complains about this or that, she feels like a quarrelsome nag. She underestimates her own rights and her power to make a start at changing things. According to Dr. Harris, she's going to have to be the one to take stock of the total situation and to blow the whistle.

"There are hundreds of thousands of guys like Charlie," Dr. Harris said. "For some reason many of them don't feel acceptable enough. They are anxious to have the approval of their male peer group," he explained. "People like Charlie reinforce each other. They fear putting the relationship with 'the guys' in jeapordy, but they're embarked on a collision course with disaster as far as family is concerned."

He pointed out that a man like Charlie doesn't want his marriage to be in trouble, either, because the marriage satisfies his dependency needs. "Mrs. Charlie Spender may have to take the initiative. She may lose. However, there is a reasonable chance of success — fairly good if she persists. I recommend she try the action course and get Charlie involved as a partner in their search for improvement."

What might happen with people like Norm and Shirley Proper?

Dr. Harris expressed a great deal of enthusiasm for the future prospects of people in similar circumstances. I share that enthusiasm. If dutiful spenders like the Propers can come to understand what they've been doing, they can change. They can, in partnership, create a marvelous new life.

Such a transformation as Norm and Shirley Proper might achieve requires the participation of both partners. If one sets out to explore life's opportunities and the other remains in the position of dutifully going along, this won't be an enjoyable or workable arrangement. It seems to me that a couple like Norm and Shirley, who have faced much of life together, stand an excellent chance of embarking on a new and adventurous course. But how can they withdraw the support their children might have become accustomed to?

"They might consider what course of action they would take with their children if some physical problem prevented them from maintaining their present level of support," Dr. Harris said. "Neither of them need feel they have to apologize to their children." People like the Propers have been taught to feel guilty if they indulge themselves instead of their children. They can, of course, scale down their contributions gradually to a more realistic level. There's another point. I suspect that many children of overly dutiful parents may feel greatly relieved if they are freed from the burden of being grateful. They may miss a few of the amenities, but they may be delighted at the freedom to sink or swim on their own.

Imagine what might happen if Norm and Shirley decided to pursue their dreams. I've had a great deal of fun plotting various futures for them. Let's explore my favorite.

Suppose that Norm tries out his penchant for going to sea under sail. He discovers that he really likes sailing, as well as puttering around to keep his boat in shape. However, he does not enjoy being a solitary sailor. He likes to have people around with whom he can talk over ideas and share enthusiasms.

I think that Shirley would at first have a great deal of difficulty abandoning the idea that she should provide support for every undertaking of Norm's. So she helps him with his new boat a few times, but she really doesn't enjoy it. After they talk over this experience, she decides to venture into the world of local politics.

A woman she knows is running for city council, and Shirley plunges into a round of activity to help her friend's campaign. She finds that while she is intrigued with the interactions among people, she really has little taste for the endless rounds of mailing campaign literature, knocking on doors, and going to fundraisers.

After a time, and some very careful consideration of both their finances and their personal inclinations, the Propers decide to follow Norm's dream. The year their son graduates from high school Norm sells the accounting business and invests in a venture running charter excursions by sail from a Baja California resort. Shirley discovers, while she is helping him get the business started, that she has a real flair for putting together the brochures that will promote it.

I see them five years down the road.

Norm's charter venture, well capitalized with the proceeds from the sale of his business, is prospering. Shirley, having done so well with the photography and writing for his brochures and some publicity articles, now finds herself in a modest career as a writer.

They've got a house in a Mexican seaport town; it is small but charming and arranged to their liking. Shirley particularly enjoys the view of bright bougainvillea blooming in the courtyard outside the room she uses for her writing office.

Their children, as excited as they about the new ventures, look forward to visiting during vacations. For very good reasons they regard their parents as especially interesting and unusual people.

While Norm accompanies expeditions for naturalists and photographers aboard the forty-foot yacht, Shirley usually remains ashore. They've both found time to be active in the affairs of the American community in the little town, and her articles on the region are selling well. What's more, she has begun the outline of a novel based on the interactions of American and Mexican citizens in a small coastal town.

May all of the Norm and Shirley Propers of this world follow their dreams, whatever they are and wherever they lead. This, indeed, is "the last of life, for which the first was made."

Whatever your situation, and whatever course you embark upon, may you be successful.

Complete Set
of Worksheets

WHAT I DREAM OF

1.

2.

3.

4.

5.

6.

7.

8.

9.

10.

CATEGORIZED LIST OF OBJECTIVES

CATEGORY ONE: SECURITY

(Objectives—employment, retirement, obligations.)

1.

2.

3.

4.

5.

6.

7.

8.

9.

10.

(Means to achieve objectives—debt reduction, investments, rentals, etc.)

1.

2.

3.

4.

5.

6.

7.

8.

9.

10.

CATEGORY TWO: CARING FOR OTHERS

(Voluntary altruistic wishes, including church, college, community, or personal charity.)

1.

2.

3.

4.

5.

6.

7.

8.

9.

10.

CATEGORY THREE: BUYABLES

(Consumer durables, real estate, vacations—just about everything that is advertised for sale.)

1.

2.

3.

4.

5.

6.

7.

8.

9.

10.

11.

12.

13.

14.

15.

CATEGORY FOUR: LEISURE

(Services to buy, things to learn for fun, hobbies, time for people.)

1.

2.

3.

4.

5.

6.

7.

8.

9.

10.

11.

12.

13.

14.

15.

MONTHLY AUDIT Time period: _____

CASH

NOT CASH

Total cash _____

Total installments _____

Total interest _____

Total debt still due _____

WORKSHEET FOR SIX-MONTH PLANNING

Item	Roots Review	Substitution?	Timing

SIX-MONTH ANALYSIS: STEP ONE

MONTH	CASH TOTAL	NOT-CASH TOTAL	INSTALLMENTS	INTEREST	DEBT
_____					
_____					
_____					
_____					
_____					
_____					

SIX-MONTH ANALYSIS: STEP TWO

MONTH	SIGNIFICANT AMOUNT	SPENDING ITEM	QUESTIONS/INSIGHTS

REVISED LIST OF OBJECTIVES (Name _____)

SOURCE			CATEGORY	ITEM
Own	Joint	Part.		

MERGED LIST OF OBJECTIVES

CATEGORY	SHARED OBJECTIVES	INDIVIDUAL OBJECTIVES

SPENDING PROJECTION

ESTIMATED COST   ITEM   TIMING

MONTHLY PLAN AND AUDIT

CATEGORY   ESTIMATE ACTUAL AMOUNT

INCOME

  Salary

  Other sources

  Total

ROUTINE SPENDING

  Cash

  Not Cash

  Extra installment payment

  Total

AVAILABLE FOR
SIGNIFICANT SPENDING

PLANNED SIGNIFICANT SPENDING

_____

_____

_____

UNPLANNED SIGNIFICANT SPENDING

_____

_____

_____

TOTAL SIGNIFICANT SPENDING

BOTTOM LINE SUMMARY: Total Income for Month _____
Total Spent During Month _____
Installment Debt Balance _____